Developing Early
Science Skills Outdoors

Activity ideas and best practice for teaching and learning outside

by Marianne Sargent

Dedication

Thank you as always to my husband Ged and fantastic little boy Harry who try so hard to give me time and space to write during breaks from model brick building!

Acknowledgements

Thanks must go to Peter Lambert, Vicki Cawthorn and the children at Chinley Primary School, High Peak, Derbyshire for inviting me in to the reception class to join in with their outdoor activities and allowing the use of a number of photographs.

· ·

Published by Practical Pre-School Books, A Division of MA Education Ltd, St Jude's Church, Dulwich Road, Herne Hill, London, SE24 0PB.

Tel: 020 7738 5454 www.practicalpreschoolbooks.com

Associate Publisher: Angela Morano Shaw

© MA Education Ltd 2015

Design: Alison Coombes **fonthill**creative 01722 717043

All images © MA Education Ltd. All photos taken by Lucie Carlier or Ben Suri, with the exception of the following: p.1 (right), p.6, p.10, p.16, p.22 (bottom left), p.25, p.26, p.29, p.34, p.38, p.41, p.42 (bottom right), p.54, p.57, p.61, p.69 and p.74 taken by Marianne Sargent. Photos on p.45 (bottom left), p.46 (top left) and p.70 © Marianne Sargent.

ISBN 978-1-909280-84-7

Developing Early Science Skills Outdoors

by Marianne Sargent

Contents

Introduction

About the series

This series is intended for early years students and practitioners working with children aged two to five years. It aims to demonstrate how outdoor provision is just as important as the indoor classroom and highlight the wealth of opportunities the outdoor environment provides for teaching basic skills and concepts in maths, science and literacy.

In her review of the Early Years Foundation Stage (EYFS) in England, Dame Tickell (2011) recommended a focus on 'how children learn rather than what they learn'. She identified three characteristics of effective learning; playing and exploring, active learning and creating and thinking critically. The books in this series outline the basic concepts and skills that underpin maths, science and literacy and show how the outdoor environment promotes an active, social and exploratory pedagogical approach to early learning.

Dame Tickell also singled out three 'prime' areas of learning; communication and language, personal, social and emotional development, and physical development. She identified these as fundamentally important for laying secure foundations in preparation for more formal education.

Therefore, these books promote early years practice that:

- Involves active practical activities that prompt lively debate and conversation, enabling children to develop the communication and language skills they need to find out about the world and make sense of new information, as well as discuss, extend and evaluate ideas;

- Gives children the chance to practise large and fine motor control, which is not only essential for cognitive development, but important in terms of gaining the strength and co-ordination needed for future writing and recording;

- Fosters physical and playful activity, promoting healthy personal, social and emotional development by reducing stress, improving mood and boosting motivation and learning.

The books contain a wealth of ideas for enhancing continuous outdoor provision, as well as planning focussed maths, science and literacy activities that exploit the unique qualities of the outdoor environment. They also provide advice on planning and assessment, where to find resources and recommendations for further reading. Throughout each book there are links to all four British early years curricula.

Developing Science Outdoors

It is through active social early years experiences that children eventually become capable of logical, creative and critical thought. The outdoor environment facilitates active and physical exploration of the world, where children learn and use language to make sense of what they encounter. They do this in an unrestricted space that allows for vocal discussion and argument, which extends their knowledge and helps them to form new thinking and ideas.

Early years pioneers Jerome Bruner (1966) and Jean Piaget (1952) advocate physical exploration that helps children to develop understanding of basic concepts. They believe children internalise the knowledge they gain through hands-on experience and this later leads to more complex abstract thought.

This theory is supported by the hugely influential Researching Effective Pedagogy in the Early Years (REPEY) and Effective Provision of Pre-school Education (EPPE) research projects, which advocate planning practical experiences for children to 'actively construct conceptual knowledge' (Siraj-Blatchford et al, 2002) through a balance of taught and 'freely chosen yet potentially instructive child-initiated activities' (Siraj-Blatchford et al, 2004).

It is extremely important that young children gain first-hand experience of scientific phenomena. It is only through personal exploration that children will develop a secure understanding of how the world works. Otherwise they are at risk of developing superficial knowledge, leading to misconception and delayed later learning. The outdoor environment is the ideal arena for scientific enquiry. When outside children are able to investigate a wide range of human processes and natural occurrences. They can observe living things, examine an abundance of materials and experience change.

Furthermore, when outside children are less restricted and have the freedom to move around and make a mess.

Outside, children have the space to carry out large scale experiments, for example by flying kites and building water rafts; they engage in messy play to find out how different materials feel, change and behave, such as water and ice, wet clay and dry sand; and they have direct access to the natural elements, through which they can explore natural phenomena including freezing, melting, evaporation, growth and decay.

Lev Vygotsky (1986) further highlights the role of social interaction in learning. It is his contention that children extend and develop their thinking through discussion with more knowledgeable others. This is again supported by the REPEY and EPPE research, which identify the need for good quality verbal interactions that extend and develop thinking. All four British early years curricula place much emphasis on the importance of children developing a wide vocabulary that enables them to talk about and describe their observations and experiences.

The outdoor environment promotes active social learning, which is essential for acquiring early scientific enquiry skills and developing an understanding of scientific concepts. It is the ideal arena for children to observe and explore, discuss findings, test theories against others and develop ever more accurate ideas. There is no need to be quiet outside in the open, where noise is carried away on the breeze.

Laying the Foundations for a successful future

The Effective Pre-school, Primary and Secondary Education (EPPSE 3-16) project report outlines how crucial the REPEY and EPPE research findings are. The report summarises the findings of the entire longitudinal study, which followed nearly 2,600 children from their early years through to the age of 16 and aimed 'to explore the most important influences on developmental pathways that lead to GCSE achievement, mental well-being, social behaviours and aspirations for the future'.

EPPSE reports that children who attended pre-school achieved 'higher total GCSE scores and higher grades in GCSE English and maths'. What's more, attending a high quality setting, where children are exposed to active, social learning experiences, was most beneficial and 'significantly predicted total GCSE scores as well as English and maths grades'. This was also a determining factor in terms of following an academic route into A levels, showing 'that the benefits of pre-school in shaping long term outcomes remain across all phases of schooling and last into young adulthood' (Sylva et al., 2014).

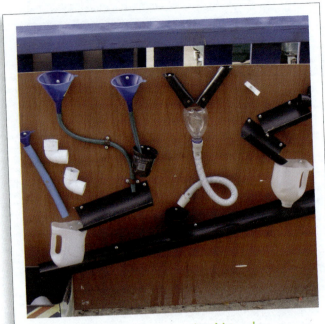

Science in the early years should involve purposeful outdoor learning experiences where children can investigate first-hand.

The great outdoors

Outdoor provision is a fundamental aspect of early years education and is a statutory requirement across all four early years curricular. The EYFS (DfE, 2014) states practitioners should provide flexible indoor and outdoor spaces where children can access stimulating resources that promote active exploration and play, while all the time being supported by knowledgeable adults who encourage them to think and ask questions.

The Scottish Curriculum for Excellence (SCE) promotes the outdoors as 'significant' to learning in literacy, numeracy and health and wellbeing, crediting it with helping young children 'make connections experientially, leading to deeper understanding within and between curriculum areas' (LTS, 2010).

The Welsh Foundation Phase Framework (WFPF) sets out the requirement that 'children should as far as possible be able to move freely between the indoors and outdoors' (DCELLS, 2008). Supporting guidance advocates play and 'first-hand experiences' as fundamentally important for the development of language, concentration, concepts and skills 'that will support their future learning' (DCELLS, 2008a).

Furthermore, the Northern Ireland Curricular Guidance for Pre-School Education (NIC) identifies outdoor learning as 'an integral part of the overall educational programme' and promotes a 'planned, purposeful, flexible' approach to teaching and learning where children should be given 'opportunities to explore,

experiment, plan and make decisions for themselves' (CCEA, 2006). This is further supported in the Primary Curriculum, which promotes play as the main vehicle for learning in the foundation stage because 'children learn best when learning is interactive, practical and enjoyable' (CCEA, 2007).

Learning in the early years is about gaining the fundamental knowledge and skills that provide the basis for future learning. The outdoor environment is an ideal arena for teaching early maths, science and literacy because it offers scope to plan concrete experiences in purposeful contexts, helping children to develop a basic conceptual understanding of these subjects.

About this book

Developing Early Science Skills Outdoors is divided into sections that represent the following methods of scientific enquiry:

- Observing

- Exploring

- Comparing, sorting and classifying

- Gathering information

- Questioning

- Investigating

- Following instructions

- Measuring

- Hypothesising

- Predicting

- Coming up with ideas

- Problem solving

- Recording

- Interpreting

- Reflecting and evaluating

- Presenting

- Using technology.

Each of these methods is introduced with an explanation of why it is important, together with an overview of the fundamental concepts and skills that underpin it. This is followed up with:

- Ideas for adult-led and adult-initiated outdoor activities that aim to develop basic scientific enquiry skills through the study of the three scientific disciplines: biology, chemistry and physics.

- Suggestions for how to enhance continuous outdoor provision so that it promotes the use of each method of scientific enquiry during child-initiated and child-led activity and play.

- General reminders and tips about teaching early science skills, as well as ideas for how to involve parents.

- The main areas of learning addressed in the English, Scottish, Welsh and Northern Irish early years curriculum frameworks.*

At the end of the book there is advice on planning and organising outdoor learning with suggestions for how to make the most of different sized outside spaces. This is followed by guidance on how to collect evidence of children's learning with practical tips for observing outdoors and pointers for how to make observation less onerous. Furthermore, there is an example observation sheet together with advice on the effective use of observations to inform assessment and future planning.

Finally, there is a list of suppliers where many of the resources used for activities throughout the book can be found, as well as links to useful websites and suggestions for further reading about teaching and learning science outdoors.

There is a large body of contemporary research highlighting the benefits of learning outdoors. Helen Bilton (2010) provides a summary:

Physical development

Research highlights links between physical exercise and cognitive development. Exercise increases the ability of blood cells to absorb oxygen and this has a positive knock-on effect for physical brain function.

Health and wellbeing

There is evidence to suggest that spending time outside in the fresh air helps to reduce illness, such as coughs and colds. Furthermore, sunlight activates vitamin D within the body, which is essential for healthy bone growth. Vitamin D can help reduce the chance of cancer and heart disease, which are also linked to sedentary lifestyles. When children are outside they are more active and get more physical exercise, which has health benefits for later life. What's more, exercise reduces stress and improves mood, which in turn boosts motivation and learning.

Learning

Studies highlight the importance of daylight and fresh air for effective learning. Many classrooms have unhealthy levels of carbon dioxide, which impacts upon children's concentration and memory. Children are more able to hear teachers and each other when they are in open spaces, making a quieter outdoor environment more conducive to learning than a noisy classroom. Furthermore, the outdoor environment is more physically challenging and this presents children with opportunities to weigh up physical risk in relation to their own capabilities. Such skills are transferable and applicable to emotional risk, giving children the courage to take on academic and philosophical challenges.

*Although the SCE identifies science as a specific curriculum area, the EYFS places science within 'understanding the world', the NIC places it within 'the world around us' and in the WFPF science can be found under 'knowledge and understanding of the world'. Therefore, the curriculum links throughout this book are primarily drawn from these areas of learning. However, science also involves the use of communication and language skills, as well as personal and social skills, and aspects of mathematics and creative development. Therefore, many learning outcomes are selected from across these areas also. Where this is the case the area of learning is indicated in brackets.

Research shows that spending time outdoors has a positive effect on children's physical development, health, well-being and general learning.

Observing

Children who are encouraged to look closely at the world around them develop a sense of curiosity, which motivates them to want to find out more. Furthermore, giving children opportunities to observe objects and living things helps them to develop a basic underlying knowledge of what the world is constructed of and how things work.

This means learning the vocabulary and language needed to name objects and living things, as well as to label features and describe happenings. It also means being encouraged to hone in on individual details and identify similarities and differences.

Observation involves the following skills:

- Being curious about the features of the natural and man-made environment

- Being able to identify places, objects, materials and living things

- Being able to describe the features of places, objects, materials and living things

- Being able to make comparisons and identify similarities and differences

- Being able to find links between different pieces of information.

In the early years children should be provided with opportunities to observe a wide range of natural and humanly-constructed phenomena. Of course, the outdoor environment provides an abundance of both. The following activities aim to spark an interest and get children looking closely at everything around them.

Activity 1: Busy spinners

Type of activity: Adult-led, small groups.

Resources: Magnifying glasses, digital camera.

What to do: Take the children out early on a dewy autumn morning to look for spider webs. Stop to look closely at each one. Ask the children to describe the structure of the web. Do they know how spiders spin them? Encourage the children to look closely at the webs and spiders using magnifying glasses. Can they describe what they see? Watch the spiders working and encourage the children to name their features and talk about how they move. Take photographs, print and laminate them to display.

Key vocabulary: Spider, legs, body, head, eyes, crawl, web, spin, dew, pattern.

Extension ideas: Use information books and the internet to find close up images of spiders and find out why and how they spin webs.

Find some spider webs and spend time watching the spiders.

Activity 3: Salt sparkle art

Type of activity: Adult-initiated, during independent play.

Resources: Black sugar paper, paint brushes, salt, bucket, plastic tubs, food colouring.

What to do: Invite the children to help mix a large amount of salt into a bucket of warm water. Once the salt has dissolved, pour the solution into several bowls and add different coloured food colouring to each one.

Give the children black sugar paper for them to paint on with the coloured salt water solutions. Put the pictures out in the sun to dry and watch the water evaporate to reveal coloured sparkly salt pictures.

Key vocabulary: Water, salt, dissolve, mix, colour, dry, evaporate, sparkle, shine.

Extension ideas: Invite children to dip fingers into clean salted and sugared water and taste the difference.

Activity 2: Then and now

Type of activity: Adult-led, small groups.

Resources: Strips of black card, double-sided sticky tape, scissors, natural materials, digital camera.

What to do: Take the children outside in late summer and ask them to collect some natural objects such as leaves, seeds, twigs and flowers. Give each child a strip of card with a piece of double-sided sticky tape stuck across the centre. Invite the children to stick their objects along the strip on the card. Talk about the children's collections. Help them identify and name the objects and encourage them to describe how they look, smell and feel. Mount the strips on a display board, take a photo of each strip and save it for later.

After several weeks, print off the photos and take the strips down from the display. Then bring the children together to compare the photo with the strip as it looks now. Encourage the children to describe the differences they can see. Allow them to touch and smell the objects on the strip and ask them if they notice any difference in how the objects feel and smell. Can any of the children explain what has happened to the objects?

Key vocabulary: Leaf, green, brown, soft, dry, brittle, seed, round, hard, flower, colours, shrivelled, dead, decayed, rotten.

Extension ideas: Pick fruits, leave them to decay and observe what happens.

Take a closer look at snow.

Activity 4: Snow close up

Type of activity: Adult-led, small groups.

Resources: Magnifying glasses.

What to do: Explain snow is water that is frozen into tiny ice crystals. These crystals bump into each other in the air and join together to form snow flakes. Once the snow flakes are heavy enough they fall to the ground.

Invite the children to pick up handfuls of snow and look at it closely. Can they see all the little crystals? Encourage them to squeeze the snow in their hands and describe what happens. What does it feel and sound like? What happens to it when it is crushed together and rolled into a ball?

Key vocabulary: Snow, snowflake, crystal, shine, sparkle, squeeze, crush, crunch, smooth, melt, freeze, frozen.

Extension ideas: Find close up images of snowflakes on the internet.

Try...

...setting up a digital microscope indoors for children to bring in the things they find outside and look at them in even greater detail.

Activity 5: On the farm

Type of activity: Whole group visit.

Resources: Transport and adult supervision for a trip off-site.

What to do: Take the children to a farm. Look at the different animals and ask the children to name and describe their features. Look at where the animals live and find out what they eat. Watch how the animals move and interact with each other.

Key vocabulary: Farm animals, legs, udder, ears, nose, trotters, hooves, feathers, wings, beak, tail, horns.

Extension ideas: Taste farm produce and find out which animal it comes from.

Activity 6: Up close

Type of activity: Adult-led, during independent play.

Resources: Child-friendly digital cameras.

What to do: Take extreme close-up photos of natural and man-made objects with the children. Zoom in on natural items such as the bark of a tree, different flowers, a grassy patch and the back of a leaf. Help the children take highly focused snaps of minibeasts. Get pictures of man-made objects such as bricks, the scraped bottom of a plastic sand/water tray and a planed plank of wood from a bench. While you are taking the photos, encourage the children to point out details and describe the colours, shapes and patterns they can see.

Key vocabulary: Colour, shape, pattern, crack, hole, wood, plastic, stone, concrete, brick, sand, cement, rot, smooth, rough, spotted, move, crawl, bent, scratch.

Extension ideas: Print off and display the photos on the inside of windows facing out. Can other children identify what each picture is?

Build your own minibeast hotel.

Enhancing continuous provision

Provide child-friendly digital cameras and magnifying glasses to encourage children to observe objects and creatures more closely. Print off and laminate information cards that will help children to identify flowers, insects and birds. Join the children, talk with them and introduce vocabulary to help them describe what they see.

Area of provision	Enhancements that encourage children to observe
Water	Place large pieces of coloured ice in the water tray for the children to watch melt. Line the bottom of a deep tray with soil and place some large rocks in it. Leave it to fill with rain water then add some pond plants and wait for wildlife to move in. Draw children's attention to reflections in puddles (and windows and shiny objects).
Sand	Build a large sandcastle and put a barrier around it for the children to watch it erode and collapse over time. Provide magnifiers for the children to examine grains of sand up close.
Construction	On a breezy day, set up some structures using various construction materials such as wooden and plastic bricks, stones and rocks. Attach roofs made of card, paper, wood and plastic on the structures and leave them for the children to observe what happens.
Role Play	Allotment: Set up a shed or tent filled with gardening tools. Allocate a patch of soil or provide planters, compost, seeds and bulbs for the children to plant, cultivate and watch grow.
Investigation	Set up a vivarium indoors to house different minibeasts in turn. Create a display for each creature with information cards, close up photographs and plastic toy examples. Place a range of metal (iron, steel, tin, copper and aluminium) objects such as keys, nails, paperclips and coins in a tray and leave them outside in all weathers for the children to observe what happens to the different metals.
Physical	Provide balloons, windmills, flags and streamers for children to run around and watch float, rotate and trail in the breeze. Display a child-sized 'my body' poster on the inside of a window facing out. Use a poster that shows the inner workings of the human body, including the heart, lungs, muscles, veins and arteries.
Garden	Lay out a picnic blanket with storybooks about nature, such as *The Very Busy Spider* by Eric Carle and *Jasper's Beanstalk* by Nick Butterworth. Use wooden pallets, old pieces of tile and slate, old carpet, bamboo, grass turf, plant pots, dry leaves and compost to set up a minibeast hotel (see photo opposite). Wait for the insects to move in and provide bug collectors and magnifiers for the children to collect and study them. Set up a bird table in a quiet spot so the children can watch the birds feed out of reach. Draw some large cloud shapes on the floor with playground chalk and invite the children to lie inside them on their backs and watch the sky.

Curriculum links

Using observation skills covers the following areas of learning and development:

EYFS	Looks closely at similarities, differences, patterns and change; talks about the features of their own immediate environment and how environments might vary from one another; makes observations of animals and plants, and talks about changes (UW). Extends vocabulary, especially by grouping and naming, exploring the meaning and sounds of new words (CL).
NIC	Shows curiosity about living things, places, objects and materials in the environment; identifies similarities and differences between living things, places, objects and materials; is aware of the local natural and built environment and their place in it (WAU). Names, describes and uses a growing vocabulary (LL).
SCE	Develops curiosity and understanding of the environment and our place in the living, material and physical world; has observed living things in the environment over time and is becoming aware of how they depend on each other; enjoys taking photographs to represent experiences and the world (S). Extends and enriches vocabulary through listening, talking and watching (LE).
WFPF	Is curious and finds out by making observations; describes what they have found out and offers simple explanations; makes comparisons and identifies similarities and differences (KUW). Extends vocabulary through activities that encourages interest in words (LLC).

Exploring

As already mentioned, observation is the most fundamental method of scientific enquiry. For young children observation is a hands-on activity and involves exploring objects, materials and living things with all five senses. This multi-sensory exploration helps children to identify, classify and discriminate between different objects and materials. This leads to understanding about relationships and how things work.

Again, vocabulary and language are an extremely important part of this and children should be encouraged to share their thoughts and ideas as they explore.

Exploration involves the following skills:

- Being curious about the features of the natural and man-made environment

- Being able to identify objects, materials and living things

- Being able to use all five senses (sight, hearing, smell, touch and taste) to explore objects, materials and living things in order to identify features and make comparisons

- Being able to describe the visual features of objects, materials and living things, as well as sounds, smells, textures and tastes

- Being able to find links between different pieces of information.

The outdoor environment is an assault on the senses. Children are presented with a wide range of natural and humanly-constructed objects and materials that are ever changing as a result of the weather and revolving seasons.

Activity 1: Creepy crawlies

Type of activity: Adult-led, small groups.

Resources: Bug catchers.

What to do: Help the children capture some minibeasts. Talk about being gentle and taking care not to hurt these small fragile creatures.

Encourage one child at a time to choose a minibeast to place on the flat palm of their hand. Ask the children to describe how the creatures move and what they feel like when they travel across their hands. Talk about the features of the different minibeasts in relation to how they move.

Key vocabulary: Woodlouse, spider, beetle, crawl, scuttle, scurry, fast, slow, legs, feet, slug, snail, worm, foot, smooth, slimy, sticky, wriggle, tickle.

Extension ideas: Take the children to a large space and encourage them to move like different minibeasts.

Find out what it feels like to have a minibeast wriggle on your hand.

Don't forget to think about...

...setting up activities and experiences that appeal to the children's sense of smell, as this sense is often overlooked. Ideas include adding food essence to sand and water and planting flowers with strong scents.

Activity 3: Barefoot trail

Type of activity: Adult-initiated, during independent play.

Resources: Bowl filled with warm soapy water, towels, long shallow trays, sand, gravel, dry and wet leaves, grass turf, mud, pebbles.

What to do: Arrange some long shallow trays in a row to make a barefoot trail. Line the bottoms of the trays with a range of natural materials.

Invite children to take off their shoes and socks and walk along the trail. Encourage them to describe how the different materials feel under their feet.

Key vocabulary: Sand, rough, gravel, sharp, pebbles, smooth, bumpy, leaves, wet, slimy, dry, crunchy, grass, soft, springy, mud, gooey, sloppy.

Extension ideas: Allow the children to add other materials to the trail.

Activity 2: Sensory scavenger hunt

Type of activity: Adult-led, during independent play.

Resources: A4 paper, printer, clipboards, pencils, small baskets.

What to do: Some settings may need to visit a local park or woodland area to do this activity.

Type up a list of objects that can be found in the outdoor area. For each object provide a sensory description and a photograph. For example:

- Pointy shiny holly leaves
- Sweet smelling pink flower
- Hard smooth pebbles
- Rough cracked tree bark
- Smooth grey slate
- Flexible clear plastic
- Spiky yellow chestnut cases.

Challenge the children to find one of each object. Help them by reading out the descriptions. When the children return ask them to describe the objects they have found.

Key vocabulary: See, hear, sound, touch, feel, smell, scent, rough, smooth, hard, soft, spiky, sharp, sweet, musky, damp, cold.

Extension ideas: Help the children suggest objects with descriptions and set up a scavenger hunt for their friends.

Find out what happens when you roast marshmallows.

Activity 4: Roasting marshmallows

Type of activity: Adult-led, small groups under close supervision.

Resources: Large stones, dry wood, kindling, safety matches, bricks, long skewer or marshmallow roasting fork, marshmallows, bucket of water (to extinguish the fire quickly).

What to do: Make a campfire: Arrange some large stones in a circle and place some dry wood in the centre. Use kindling and matches to light the fire. Use bricks to mark out a parameter circle to stop the children going too close. Give each child a cold marshmallow. Ask them to describe the texture and smell before eating it and describing its taste. Roast some marshmallows and talk about the smell. Give them to the children to eat and ask them to describe how the texture and taste have changed.

Key vocabulary: Marshmallow, spongy, soft, smooth, cook, warm, heat, hot, melt, swell, shrivel, sweet, sticky, runny.

Extension ideas: Melt marshmallows on hot chocolate and compare what happens.

Try…

…adding different substances and materials to the sand and water to change the appearance, texture and smell. Otherwise fill the trays with something different altogether.

Activity 5: Dark den

Type of activity: Adult-initiated, during independent play.

Resources: Play tent, wendyhouse or play shed, blackout fabric, thick blankets or black sugar paper, pegs, torches, battery operated fibre optics, tinfoil, plastic mirrors, glow-in-the-dark shapes, glitter ball.

What to do: Lay some glow-in-the-dark shapes in the daylight to 'charge up'. Set up a play tent or wendyhouse, drape some blackout fabric over the top and secure it with pegs. Otherwise black out the windows of a play shed with black sugar paper. Attach shiny and glowing objects to the walls and ceiling.

Provide torches for the children to go inside and explore. When they come out ask them to tell you how it felt being in the dark den and what they saw. What did it feel like when they came back out again? How did it affect their eyes?

Key vocabulary: Dark, black, light, shine, glitter, sparkle, glow, glare.

Extension ideas: Ask the children to find more objects to put inside the den.

Activity 6: Brambling

Type of activity: Adult-led, whole group, later divided into small groups.

Resources: Information books about fruit, plastic containers, baskets, enough adults for an off-site trip.

What to do: Share some information books about fruit. Look at examples of different types of berry such as strawberries, blackberries, raspberries, blueberries and gooseberries. Talk about safety when it comes to wild berry picking. Ensure the children understand they should never eat a berry that they do not recognise.

Go out blackberry picking. Explain blackberry bushes have thorns to stop scavengers from stealing the fruit. Squash some berries, look at the juice and talk about the colour and smell. Eat some and talk about the taste.

Key vocabulary: Blackberry, fruit, smell, taste, squash, juice, colour, thorn, sharp, seeds.

Extension Ideas: Use the fruit to make blackberry and apple pie.

Enhancing continuous provision

Encourage children to use all of their senses by providing a range of objects and materials for them to explore during independent play. It is important that children are exposed to both natural and man-made materials. Help them to distinguish between the two by setting up challenges that encourage them to explore the different properties of each. Lead on from this by helping the children to consider the relationship between the properties of each material and how it is used.

Area of provision	Enhancements that encourage children to explore
Water	Fill the water tray with jelly, soap-flake slime, wet couscous, cornflour and water mix, ice cubes, shaving foam and wet porridge oats. Add objects and substances to the water such as sponges, flannels, shredded paper, cotton wool, dry pasta shapes, washing up liquid and oil.
Sand	Fill the sand tray with dry coloured rice, pasta, pulses, cereals, coffee grounds and flax seed. Add objects and substances to the sand such as water, washing up liquid, plastic and metal coins, glass pebbles, glitter and shells.
Construction	Set out two large containers and stick a label of a person on one and a label of a flower on the other. Provide a selection of objects made out of natural and man-made materials such as a wooden block, small red brick, smooth piece of slate, bag of sand, metal door handle and some plastic toy tools. Write on the floor in chalk, Sort the building materials into natural and man-made.
Role Play	Home decor store: Turn a playhouse or shed into home decor store. Provide carpet, lino and wallpaper samples and stick some tiles to a piece of wood for children to examine and choose from. Provide home decorating catalogues and brochures for the children to flick through.
Investigation	Make a set of feely boxes and put natural objects inside for the children to examine and identify. Allow the children to replace the objects for others of their own choosing. Provide magnets for the children to carry around the outdoor area and test on different materials. Explore the properties of clay by heating some up and adding water to it.
Physical	Provide voice changers and wireless microphones for children to play around with the sound of their voices. Use playground chalk to draw weather symbols on the floor of a wide open space with written instructions asking children to, Move like… a gentle breeze, a strong gale, warm sun rays, falling raindrops and twirling snowflakes.
Garden	Provide large crayons and thin paper for the children to do tree and stone rubbings. Hang light catchers for the children to watch glint and sparkle in the sunshine.

Curriculum links

Exploring covers the following areas of learning and development:

EYFS	Explores objects by linking together different approaches; talks about the things they have observed, such as plants, animals, natural and found objects; looks closely at similarities, differences, patterns and change (UW). Extends vocabulary, especially by grouping and naming, exploring the meaning and sounds of new words (CL).
NIC	Identifies similarities and differences between living things, places, objects and materials; understands that different materials behave in different ways and have different properties; understands that some materials change if kept in different conditions (WAU). Names, describes and uses a growing vocabulary (LL).
SCE	Can identify senses and use them to explore the world; explores the nature of sound and light; uses musical instruments to explore the relationship between vibrations and sounds produced; explores the properties of different substances and how they can be changed (S). Extends and enriches vocabulary through listening, talking and watching (LE).
WFPF	Experiments with different everyday objects and materials and uses their senses to sort them according to simple features and properties; understands how some everyday materials change in shape when stretched, squashed, bent and twisted, and when heated or cooled; understands that light comes from a variety of sources and that darkness is the absence of light; understands that there are many kinds and sources of sound (KUW). Extends vocabulary through activities that encourages interest in words (LLC).

Comparing, sorting and classifying

Children learn how to compare, sort and classify in stages. Very young children begin by sorting objects according to their own criteria, which does not always seem logical to an outsider. They then move on to sort objects using a single criterion such as colour. As children become capable of more complex thought they begin to recognise that objects can be sorted according to more than one criterion such as colour, shape and material, and this makes it possible to reorganise and move items into different categories. Some young children are capable of taking this a step further by sorting objects according to two criteria at the same time, for example, picking out all the balls that are both red and bouncy from a varied selection.

Comparing, sorting and classifying involves the following skills:

- Being able to describe the features of objects, materials and living things

- Being able to make comparisons and identify similarities and differences

- Understanding and being able to use language such as 'same', 'different', 'compare' and 'sort'

- Being able to find links between different pieces of information.

Being able to compare, sort and classify is important because as children move on in their science education they will be faced with investigations that involve recognising and controlling variables in order to carry out a fair test. This means keeping some aspects of an experiment the same, while altering others to see if it has an affect. At the most basic level this involves being able to make simple comparisons and identify similarities and differences.

Activity 1: Petal portraits

Type of activity: Adult-initiated, during independent play.

Resources: Brightly coloured flowers and other natural objects, plastic mirrors.

What to do: Invite the children to create pictures of themselves using natural materials.

Get each child to look in a mirror and talk about the colour of their hair and eyes. Then send them off to collect objects that they can use to create a self-portrait.

As they create their picture encourage them to consider the shapes of the objects they have chosen and sort and categorise them in relation to their purpose. For example, the use of round objects for eyes and long thin items for hair.

Key vocabulary: Flower, conker, grass, leaf, petal, colour, eyes, hair, long, short, round, shape.

Extension ideas: Challenge the children to do portraits of their friends. Look at similarities and differences between their features.

Carefully select natural objects and use them to create portraits.

Activity 2: Classifying colours

Type of activity: Adult-led, small groups.

Resources: Different shades of coloured paper, sellotape.

What to do: Create a colour chart by sticking pieces of coloured paper together in a long strip. Choose the colours according to the time of year and try to include three shades of each. Send the children to collect natural objects and place them on the colour chart.

Bring the children together and talk about the colours they have found. Talk about which are the lightest, brightest, darkest and most dull, and look at the different shades.

Key vocabulary: Colour, dark, light, shade, bright, dull, match, same.

Extension ideas: See if the children can sort the objects on the chart according to other criteria, for example, size or shape.

Activity 3: Leaf mobiles

Type of activity: Adult-led, small groups.

Resources: Twigs, leaves, string.

What to do: Explain you are going to make leaf mobiles to hang around the outdoor area.

Send the children to collect some good length sticks and a selection of leaves. Challenge them to work together to sort the leaves into sizes and colours then thread them onto the twigs to make one mobile with small leaves, one with large leaves, one with brown leaves and another with green leaves.

(These instructions will differ according to the time of year and what is available.)

Hang the mobiles up with string.

Key vocabulary: Leaves, sort, colour, size, shape.

Extension ideas: Challenge the children to sort the leaves according to two criteria, for example, small green leaves and large brown leaves.

HOME LINKS

Print off some bird identification charts featuring birds local to your area. Send these home over a weekend and ask parents to do some bird spotting with their children. Ask them to help their children identify different species, categorise the birds according to colour and size and record how many large/small, brown/black/white birds they saw.

Compare sunflower seeds and grow them to find out what kind of flowers they produce.

Activity 4: Sunflower surprise

Type of activity: Adult-led, small groups.

Resources: Different varieties of sunflower seeds, for example, common, red velvet, valentine, harlequin and Russian giant, shallow containers, plant pots, compost, trowels and watering cans.

What to do: Empty the packets of sunflower seeds into shallow containers. Spend some time looking at the seeds and comparing their colours, sizes and patterns. Explain all the seeds are a variety of sunflower and show the children the pictures on the seed packets. Invite the children to choose a seed each and ask them what kind of sunflower they think their seed will produce. Plant the seeds, watch them grow and find out which seed produces which flower.

Key vocabulary: Sunflower, seed, pattern, colour, size, plant, grow.

Extension ideas: Compare the sunflowers. Look at the colours, count the petals and measure the heights.

Don't forget to think about...

...allowing children to categorise according to their own criteria. Get them comparing objects and deciding how they can sort them into categories.

Activity 5: Minibeast mix up

Type of activity: Adult-led, small groups.

Resources: Digital camera, printer, laminator, information books about minibeasts.

What to do: Go out looking for minibeasts and take close-up photos of those that you find. Help the children use information books to find out more about the minibeasts in the photos. List their features, for example, how many legs, eyes and antennae they have and whether they have a shell or wings. Create information cards featuring photos of the creatures with their features listed below.

Use the cards to encourage the children to compare the minibeasts, sort and categorise them according to different criteria, for example, whether they have wings, legs or a shell.

Key vocabulary: Minibeast, slug, snail, caterpillar, centipede, woodlouse, fly, bee, spider, butterfly, beetle, ladybird, worm.

Extension ideas: Make the sorting a little more difficult by categorising according to where the creatures dwell; on the floor, underground or in the air.

Activity 6: Treasure hunt

Type of activity: Adult-initiated, during independent play.

Resources: Metal detectors, pieces of jewellery and gold coins made out of metal and plastic, large metal container, large plastic container.

What to do: Bury some treasure in the sand tray or pit. Place a large metal container and large plastic container nearby. Give the children metal detectors and ask them to find and separate the metal pieces from the plastic. They should then place each item in the container made of the same material.

Key vocabulary: Metal, plastic, sort.

Extension ideas: Look more closely at the objects and encourage the children to examine the different properties of metal and plastic. Ask them how the different materials feel, sound and look.

Enhancing continuous provision

Provide resources that will encourage children to embark on their own independent explorations of a variety of materials, objects and living things. Ensure they have access to magnifiers and observation equipment that will help them examine colours, patterns and finer details more closely.

Encourage the children to think about how different things feel, look, smell and sound, and to use these as criteria for comparing, sorting and classifying. Challenge them by providing items that can be classified according to more than one criterion. Engage them in conversation and ask them to explain how and why they have separated and sorted items in particular ways.

Area of provision	Enhancements that encourage children to compare, sort and classify
Water	Provide a range of toy sea creatures for the children to sort according to colour, size or species. Provide a range of boats that can be sorted according to weight, colour, size and material.
Sand	Place tubs of mud, sand and compost in the tray. Provide scoops, bottles of water, sieves and sample containers for the children to examine and compare appearance, texture and smell. Bury a variety of coloured plastic and glass jewels in the sand and provide spades and sieves for the children to dig them up and sort them.
Construction	Provide stones, small and large gravel, pebbles and sand, along with different sized toy diggers and dumper trucks. Provide different shaped and sized wooden blocks, real bricks and cork blocks for children to build with.
Role Play	Laundrette: Provide a basket full of clothing items that can be sorted by size, colour and pattern, for example, socks, scarves, hats, gloves and T-shirts. Fill a large bowl with warm soapy water and set up a washing line with pegs for the children to wash and hang out the laundry. Household waste sorting site: Provide clean rubbish made of plastic, card, paper and metal (take care that tins have no sharp edges) for the children to sort.
Investigation	Hang different sized pots and pans and provide wooden, plastic and metal spoons. Display questions such as, Which spoon makes the loudest sound? and Which pan makes the highest note? Make rattles using plastic, card, metal and wooden containers and using beads, buttons, dried beans, rice, metal split pins and paperclips, for the children to compare materials and sounds.
Physical	Set up a variety of tents and wigwams for the children to compare the sizes and shapes of the interior spaces. Fill a large bucket with different coloured balls made of various materials. Choose balls that can be categorised in different ways, for example, by size, colour, material and whether they are bouncy.
Garden	Set up a small world farm. Make enclosures by cutting the tops and bottoms off small cardboard boxes and provide a variety of farm animals for children to sort between them. Grow more than one variety of each type of vegetable, for example, cherry and beefsteak tomatoes, runner and broad beans, white and spring onions, and white and green cucumbers. Provide bug collectors, magnifying glasses and minibeast identification cards.

Curriculum links

Comparing, sorting and classifying covers the following areas of learning and development:

EYFS	Knows about similarities and differences in relation to places, objects, materials and living things; notices and talks about detailed features of objects in their environment (UW). Extends vocabulary, especially by grouping and naming, exploring the meaning and sounds of new words (CL).
NIC	Identifies similarities and differences between living things, places, objects and materials (WAU). Names, describes and uses a growing vocabulary (LL).
SCE	Develops curiosity and understanding of the environment and their place in the living, material and physical world; can identify senses and use them to explore the world (S). Extends and enriches vocabulary through listening, talking and watching (LE).
WFPF	Makes comparisons and identifies similarities and differences; observes differences between animals and plants, different animals, different plants and between themselves and other children in order to group them (KUW). Extends vocabulary through activities that encourages interest in words (LLC).

Find out about big vehicles.

Activity 5: Big vehicles

Type of activity: Adult-led, small groups.

Resources: Adult supervision for a trip off site and transport if needed, child-friendly digital camera.

What to do: Take the children in small groups to see some big vehicles at work on a nearby construction site. Look at which jobs each vehicle is responsible for. Watch how they move and encourage the children to describe what is happening. Help the children take photos.

Return to the setting and use information books to find out more about the different types of vehicles that work on a construction site.

Key vocabulary: Vehicle, lorry, digger, truck, dumper, backhoe, lift, heavy, shift, dump, carry, dig.

Extension ideas: Use the photos and information to make a display about large construction site vehicles.

Take a trip to the seaside.

Activity 4: On record

Type of activity: Adult-led, small groups.

Resources: Hand-held recording devices, child-friendly digital cameras.

What to do: Take the children outside and instruct them to stand still and listen. Ask them to tell you all the different sounds they can hear. Move towards the source of each sound, record it and take a photo. Use the photos and recordings to create an interactive display of outdoor sounds with sound buttons (see resources at the end of the book).

Key vocabulary: Noise, sound, listen, outside, traffic, birds, aeroplane, children, wind, chimes, river, water, siren.

Extension ideas: Ask the children if there are any other outdoor sounds that they would like to hear. Search on the internet for soundbites.

Try…

…providing clipboards, paper and pencils to encourage children to record their thinking about the information they gather.

Activity 6: Seaside trip

Type of activity: Whole group visit.

Resources: Transport and adult supervision for a trip off-site, buckets, spades, fishing nets, digital camera.

What to do: Take the children on a visit to the seaside. Encourage them to look around at the coastal scenery and talk about the natural and built environment. Build sandcastles, fish in rock pools and collect natural items from the shore. Take photos of rock pool dwellers and seabirds.

On your return to the setting use information books and the internet to identify and find out about the items you found and creatures you photographed.

Key vocabulary: Sea, sand, beach, coast, cliff, bird, seagull, shell, pebble, rock, fish, rock pool, seaweed.

Extension Ideas: Visit other localities, such as the park and town centre. Encourage the children to compare and contrast the different natural and built environments.

Enhancing continuous provision

Provide resources that encourage children to seek, gather and record information independently. Print and laminate information cards to accompany outdoor activities, display posters on the inside of windows facing out and consider getting an outdoor display board. Put up an 'information tent' containing information books and tablets containing science apps. Provide mark-making materials, digital cameras and child-friendly recording devices. Below are some ideas for resources and stimuli that will encourage children to gather their own information about places, objects, materials and living things.

Area of provision	Enhancements that encourage children to gather information
Water	Display pictures of icebergs, frozen landscapes, clouds, half-empty reservoirs, rivers and floods near the water tray. Provide information books about the weather and dry and frozen climates. Provide funnels, tubes, jugs, water wheels and bottles to play with the water and find out how it behaves.
Sand	Display pictures of deserts and beaches. Provide information books about sand, beaches, deserts and dry climates. Provide spades, rakes, scoops, buckets, magnifiers and sand moulds for the children to play with and manipulate the sand to find out how it behaves.
Construction	Display pictures of builders at work, construction sites, quarries and different types of buildings. Provide information books about building and large construction vehicles. Provide construction materials in a range of sizes, materials and shapes for the children to experiment with and find out about different uses, behaviours and capabilities.
Role Play	Mobile library: Join a small cardboard box to a larger box to make a mobile library. Use the small box as the driver's compartment with a steering wheel and the larger box as the library section. Provide information books with labelled baskets to store them in, index cards with 'book title', 'date borrowed' and 'please return by', and a date stamp.
Investigation	Set up outdoor interactive displays based around topical themes. Provide information books, photos, posters, fact cards, objects and magnifiers for the children to gather information about the subject. Leave scraps of paper with pens and pencils, as well as child-friendly digital cameras and small hand-held recording devices to encourage children to gather and record their own information.
Physical	Provide hula hoops, balls, skittles, stilts, skipping ropes, beanbags and rackets made in a variety of sizes, shapes and materials, for children to experiment with and find out how the different items behave when manipulated and moved in particular ways.
Garden	Provide child-friendly digital cameras for the children to take photos of things they see in the garden area. Provide binoculars and information cards and pocket guides about birds for the children to do some bird watching. Set up an MP3 player and play bird and animal sounds. Provide pictures and information books about garden animals for the children to use when trying to figure out which animal is making which sound.

Curriculum links

Gathering information covers the following areas of learning and development:

EYFS	Makes observations of objects, materials and living things and talks about why things happen and how things work; talks about changes; selects and uses technology for particular purposes (UW). Knows that information can be retrieved from books and computers (L).
NIC	Shows curiosity about living things, places, objects and materials in the environment; understands that different materials behave in different ways, have different properties and can be used for different purposes; is aware of everyday uses of technological tools (WAU). Browses and chooses books for a specific purpose (LL).
SCE	Develops curiosity and understanding of the environment and our place in the living, material and physical world (S). Uses signs, books or other texts to find useful or interesting information and uses this to learn new things (LE). Accesses information from electronic sources to support, enrich or extend learning; enjoys taking photographs or recording sound to represent experiences and the world (T).
WFPF	Is curious and finds out by making observations; describes what they have found out and offers simple explanations; engages with resources from a variety of contexts including interactive forms (KUW). Experiences and responds to information and reference texts including print and computer-based materials (LLC).

Questioning

Questioning is the bedrock of scientific inquiry. Science is all about raising questions and seeking answers, something that young children have the natural inclination to do. However, deciding specifically what one wants to find out and formulating productive questions that lead to deeper focused inquiry are difficult skills to learn.

Questioning involves the following skills and concepts:

- Being curious about the features of the natural and man-made environment

- Understanding what a question is and how it can be used to further learning

- Knowing how to formulate a question using enquiry words such as 'how', 'why', 'what', 'where' and 'when'

- Being able to choose and phrase a particular type of question in order to glean certain information

- Being open to new ideas.

Practitioners can help young children to develop early questioning skills by setting up provocations that appeal to their sense of wonder and curiosity. They can then support this by modelling the use of a range of questions, while encouraging children to do the same.

The outdoor environment is ideal for setting up imaginative and exciting provocations that will get children raising questions and looking for answers. All the time, engage them in thought provoking discussion and help them to formulate questions for themselves.

Activity 1: Little ice gems

Type of activity: Adult-initiated, during independent play.

Resources: Snowy weather, ice cube trays, food colouring, glitter, metallic craft shapes.

What to do: Fill some ice cube trays with water. Add colouring and sparkly materials and freeze overnight.

The following morning before the children arrive throw them into a snowy patch so they sink in. Take the children out to play in the snow and wait for them to discover the ice cubes.

Key questions: What are they? Where did they come from? What are they made of? How were they made? What do you think will happen if we leave them there?

Extension ideas: Challenge the children to make their own little ice gems.

Where did these come from?

Try…

…displaying open-ended questions on the inside of windows facing out into the outdoor area. These are useful prompts that practitioners can refer to when talking with the children and sustaining shared thinking.

Activity 3: Fake flowers

Type of activity: Adult-initiated, during independent play.

Resources: Realistic fake fabric flowers, real flowers planted in boxes or borders.

What to do: Before the children arrive at the setting go outside and insert some fake flowers amongst the real ones in the flower boxes or borders.

Invite children to help you with some weeding and wait for them to discover the fake flowers.

Key questions: How do you know they are not real? What are they made of? What is the difference between these two flowers? How do these flowers look/feel/smell compared to those? What do you think might happen if we leave them there?

Extension ideas: Leave the fake flowers in the flower bed to see what happens when the other flowers start to die off. Provide craft materials inside for the children to make their own fake flowers.

Activity 2: Shadow monsters

Type of activity: Adult-led, small groups.

Resources: Sunny weather, dark card, scissors, bamboo sticks.

What to do: Cut some monster shapes out of dark card and attach them to bamboo sticks. Take the monsters outside and stand them in the sun so that they cast a shadow. It helps if you have a soil or grass patch that you can push the stick into next to a tarmac area where the shadow will show up clearly. Otherwise snow is a great surface for making shadows. Take the children outside to look at the shadows and see if they can explain how shadows are created.

Key questions: Where do shadows come from? Can you make a shadow? How do you think a shadow is made?

Extension ideas: Allow the children to move the sticks around and see what happens to the shadows. Go out and look at the shadows later in the day to see if they have changed at all.

Don't forget to think about…

…giving children time to think. Fast-paced questioning puts off less confident children and gives others less time to formulate a considered response. Introduce 'thinking time' or 'wait time' after questions to give children a chance to think.

What might live in here?

Activity 4: Trail of twigs

Type of activity: Adult-initiated, during independent play.

Resources: Twigs, selection of natural materials.

What to do: Build a small animal house in a quiet corner using natural materials such as sticks, mud, straw, grass, moss, leaves and feathers. Lay out a trail of arrows made of twigs leading to it. Wait for the children to discover the arrows then accompany them as they follow the trail and discover the house.

Key questions: Where do you think the arrows might lead? What have you found? Have you seen anything like this before? Do you know what might live here? Why do you think that?

Extension ideas: Leave the animal house where it is and see if anything moves in.

Activity 5: Mud pie mystery

Type of activity: Adult-initiated, during independent play.

Resources: Round/dome-shaped silicone baking moulds (silicone egg poachers work), clay soil (or mud and clay), metal spoons, wooden board, round pastry cutters, metal spatula, objects to put inside.

What to do: Use a spoon to press a thick layer of mud around the inside of some dome shaped silicone baking moulds. If the soil you are using is not binding together mix some clay into it. Then spread a layer of mud onto a wooden board. Leave the moulds and wooden board somewhere warm to dry out.

When the mud is dry carefully peel off the silicone moulds and select a pastry cutter that will cut out an appropriately sized base from the sheet of mud. Put a mystery filling, for example, some glass beads, coloured rice, snail shells or straw in the centre of the round mud base. Place the mud dome over the top and seal it around the edges with more wet mud. Leave it to dry then use a metal spatula to free it from the wooden board.

Hide the mud pies around the outdoor area and wait for the children to discover them.

Key questions: What do you think it is? Where do you think it came from? What do you think might be inside? How do you think it was made?

Extension ideas: Challenge the children to make their own mud pies.

Don't forget to think about…

…the importance of creating a learning environment where children feel confident about asking questions. Reassure them that no question is daft, all contributions are valued and misunderstandings and mistakes are all part of learning.

Activity 6: Hidden ruins

Type of activity: Adult-initiated, during independent play.

Resources: Dry sand, water, PVA glue, silicone ice cube trays, sand tray, small world building site resources.

What to do: Dampen some sand with water and add some PVA glue. Mix it well and spoon it into ice cube trays. Leave it to set overnight. In an empty sand tray create a mini building ruin with the sand bricks. Use PVA glue to cement them together. Again, leave overnight to dry then pour dry sand over the top so that it is almost completely covered. Put some small world builders, trucks and tools on the sand and leave it for the children to discover.

Key questions: What have you found? What do you think the bricks are made of? How do you think they are stuck together?

Extension ideas: Provide washing up liquid, PVA glue and flour and challenge the children to make their own sand bricks.

Enhancing continuous provision

Create a questioning outdoor environment that presents children with unusual objects and scenarios that make them curious.

Appeal to their imaginations and add an element of fantasy to scientific explorations to encourage them to question what is real as opposed to make-believe. Below are some ideas for how to get children questioning and wanting to find out more.

Area of provision	Enhancements that encourage children to question
Water	Fill two buckets with bubble mixture using two different recipes. Fill the first bucket with washing-up liquid and water. Fill the second bucket with the same but add glycerin (available from chemists). Add food colouring to each bucket so that the mixtures are different colours. Provide bubble wands made from stretched out wire coat hangers (flatten and tape around the hooks to make handles). See if the children question why the bubbles containing glycerin last longer.
Sand	Create a mixture of equal parts water, cornflour and sand to make quicksand. Make a sign saying 'Beware: Quicksand!' and stick it to the side of the tray. Provide objects such as corks, pebbles, small wooden bricks and unifix cubes for the children to drop onto the surface and question why they are sinking, why some sink quicker than others and why some do not sink at all.
Construction	Use everyday materials such as rope, blankets, pegs, clothes horses and tarpaulin to make a home-made tent. Put some ruffled sleeping bags inside with an open bag of belongings. Collapse the tent and leave it for the children to discover and question what the materials were used for and what the construction was before it collapsed.
Role Play	Under the sea: Paint water effects on a piece of clear plastic sheeting; set up some clothes' airers and peg the sheeting over the top; use clear catgut (short lengths to ensure safety) to hang fish underneath; hang shredded brown and green crepe paper as seaweed; line the floor with hessian covered in sand and place some crabs and rocks. Place some information books about the ocean nearby for children to flick through while playing and imagine what it is like under the sea.
Investigation	Fill a tray with feathers. Include natural feathers from a range of birds as well as dyed feathers. Provide identification charts and books about all kinds of birds, including garden and exotic species. Pick up vehicle engine parts from scrap yards, clean them up, ensure they are safe and leave them out for the children to examine and question what they are and where they come from.
Physical	Display convex, concave and stretch and squash mirrors for children to explore and question why their appearance changes in each one. Provide trampolines and soft mats for the children to jump on and question why they can jump higher using a trampoline.
Garden	Make a carrot tree: Use clear catgut to attach carrots to the branches of a tree. Let the children discover it and question what is going on. Use playground chalk to draw wild animal footprints along the top of low walls and across the floor. Make a chart for the children featuring photos of the animals alongside their footprints. (Find a guide to mammal tracks on the Mammal Society website: www.mammal.org.uk).

Curriculum links

Questioning covers the following areas of learning and development:

EYFS	Understands and answers 'how' and 'why' questions; comments and asks questions about aspects of their familiar world such as the place where they live or the natural world; talks about why things happen and how things work (UW). Questions why things happen and gives explanations; asks who, what, when, how (CL).
NIC	Shows curiosity about the living things, places, objects and materials in the environment (WAU). Asks questions to find information or seek explanations; answers questions to give information and demonstrate understanding; offers reasons to support opinions given (LL).
SCE	Develops curiosity and understanding of the environment and their place in the living, material and physical world; develops the skills of scientific inquiry and investigation using practical techniques (S). Asks questions and links what they are learning with what they already know (LE).
WFPF	Thinks about questions and then asks them and listens to the answers; identifies what they want to find out and how to do it (KUW). Talks/communicates, spontaneously and through structured activities, for a variety of purposes, including asking and answering questions (LLC).

Investigating

Once they have had plenty of opportunities to observe, explore and gather information about a wide range of scientific phenomena children can move on to more in-depth investigation.

Unlike open-ended exploring, investigating involves an element of planning and control, usually in the form of handling variables. This means setting up more structured activities that involve changing something to see how it impacts upon how something else behaves.

Investigating involves the following skills and concepts:

- Being able to identify and describe the features of objects, materials and living things

- Being able to make comparisons and identify similarities and differences

- Understanding cause and effect (that changing something may have an affect on something else)

- Understanding the concept of a fair test

- Being able to find links between different pieces of information.

The outdoor environment makes it possible to set up exciting investigations that need space and involve making a mess. At this stage it is important to keep investigations simple. In the beginning plan investigations that involve changing just one thing. Once you have carried out some successful investigations begin asking the children for their own ideas about how to extend them by changing something else. Following are some starting points for simple outdoor investigations that introduce handling variables.

Activity 1: Escape from Hoth

Type of activity: Adult-led, small groups.

Resources: Star Wars toy figures, for example Hans Solo, Princess Leia and Luke Skywalker, three shallow containers, cornflour, shaving foam, salt, sugar, fine sand.

What to do: Stand three toy figures in a shallow containers and pour in some water. Freeze them overnight. Create a Hoth scene by filling the water tray with real snow if possible, otherwise mix a can of shaving foam with 1kg cornflour to make fake snow. Place the containers on the snow, bring the children to the scene and explain that Han Solo, Princess Leia and Luke Skywalker have been captured during the Battle of Hoth. Tell the children it is their mission to free them from the ice and rescue them with the help of salt, sugar and sand. Sprinkle the salt, sugar and sand at the base of each character and watch to see which melts the ice first. Discuss the reasons why.

Key vocabulary: Ice, frozen, water, melt, salt, sugar, sand, affect/effect, why?

Extension ideas: Try freezing water that is mixed with sugar, salt, sand and other substances to see what happens.

Set up some fun and appealing investigations.

Activity 2: Float your boat

Type of activity: Adult-led, small groups.

Resources: Small and large boat shaped silicone moulds, food colouring, water, jelly, chocolate, Plaster of Paris, clay.

What to do: Fill some small boat shaped silicone moulds with a variety of substances such as chocolate, jelly, Plaster of Paris, clay and coloured ice.

Gather the children outside at the water tray and invite them to drop the 'boats' into the water. Watch what happens and encourage the children to explain why they think some of the boats float, others sink and some hover just below the surface.

Key vocabulary: Float, sink, heavy, light, under water, on the surface, big, small, why?

Extension ideas: Make larger 'boats' using the same substances to see if they still float/sink.

Activity 3: Ice balls

Type of activity: Adult-led, small groups.

Resources: Ice ball maker, food colouring, four pieces of guttering (each the same length), bricks, tarmac, sand, gravel and grass covered surfaces.

What to do: Make a large quantity of ice balls in a range of different colours. Set up three ramps by resting the lengths of guttering on bricks, taking care to ensure the ramps are all the same height. Each ramp should lead onto a different surface such as tarmac, gravel, sand and grass.

Invite the children to roll the ice balls down the slopes. Ask them to watch what happens when the balls hit the different surfaces. Which surfaces do the balls travel furthest along? What happens to the ice when it hits and rolls across the different surfaces? How does this affect how it rolls?

Key vocabulary: Ice, ball, round, roll, slope, move, fast, slow, down, far, furthest, stop, crack, chip, melt, affect, why?

Extension ideas: Try the activity with ice cubes in different shapes and sizes.

HOME LINKS

Send home ideas for simple investigations that parents can do with their children while playing outside in the garden or at the park. For example: Find out which balls bounce the highest; Find out which toys float and sink in the paddling pool; and Find out which is the best weather for kite flying.

Go outside and investigate how physical activity affects the human body.

Don't forget to think about...

...introducing scientific language when carrying out investigations with young children. Use vocabulary such as 'fair', 'test', 'same', 'different', 'compare', 'constant', 'change', 'effect/affect' and 'measure' in your conversations with the children about what you and they are doing, while observing what happens and when discussing what to do next.

Activity 4: In a heartbeat

Type of activity: Adult-led, whole group.

Resources: A wide open space, large picture of the human body showing lungs and heart, stethoscope.

What to do: Show the children a diagram of the human body. Point to the heart and explain that it keeps them alive by pumping blood all around their bodies. Ask the children to put their hands on their chests and feel their hearts pumping. Point to the lungs and explain that they are like bags of air; when we take a breath in they fill with air and when we breathe out they empty. Ask the children to put their hands on their chests, take some deep breaths and feel their chests rise and fall as the their lungs expand and contract.

Take the children outside to a wide open space and tell them to run around for one minute. Ask them to stop, sit down and put their hands on their chests. Can they describe how they are feeling now? What is different about their heartbeats/breathing?

Key vocabulary: Heart, pump, heartbeat, faster, slower, lungs, air, breathing, expand, contract, rise, fall, change, exercise, affect/effect.

Extension ideas: Provide a working stethoscope for the children to listen to each others' hearts.

Activity 5: Zipping along

Type of activity: Adult-led, small groups.

Resources: String, long pipe cleaners, dry rigatoni pasta, small paper bag with handles, giant paperclip, marbles, digital timer.

What to do: Thread a piece of dry rigatoni pasta onto a length of string and tie the string up so that it stretches across the outdoor area on downward slope. Tie a small loop of string around through the piece of pasta. Mould a giant paperclip into an S shape and hook it onto the loop of string. Put 10 marbles in a paper bag and hang it on the hook. Release the bag so that it slides down the zip wire and use a digital timer to see how long it takes to reach the bottom. Try more or less marbles and see if the bag travels faster or slower. Discuss the reasons why.

Key vocabulary: Fast, faster, slow, slower, down, more, less, heavy, heavier, light, lighter, how long? seconds, affect/effect, why?

Extension ideas: Change the zip wire material to see if it makes a difference. Try washing line, wire, wool and catgut.

Activity 6: Under cover

Type of activity: Adult-led, small groups.

Resources: String, pegs, tinfoil, bubble wrap, greaseproof paper, tissue paper, toweling, cotton and leather fabric, bin liners, cuddly toys.

What to do: Tie two parallel lengths of string at a low level across the outdoor area. Explain you would like to create a shelter for toy characters to sit under when they are outside in the rain. Show the children the different materials and ask them which they think is most likely to keep the toys dry and why. Help the children peg the different materials on to the string. Sit some cuddly toys underneath when it rains and watch to see what happens.

Key questions: Rain, shelter, wet, dry, waterproof, leak, hole, drip, soak.

Extension ideas: Test the strength of the different materials by placing weights on the top. Test the materials when they are wet and dry and compare what happens.

Enhancing continuous provision

Provide resources and materials that encourage children to carry out their own independent investigations. Use playground chalk to write on the floor, set up an easel or leave a whiteboard next to the resources with ideas. Once the children get going allow them to run with their investigations and take them in whichever direction they choose. Help them by providing any extra resources or materials they need.

While the children are undertaking their investigations join them and engage them in conversations about what they are doing. Guide them and help them to understand the importance of choosing just one aspect of the experiment to change and compare, for example, the size, material or design of an object. Below are some examples of simple investigations that can be set up in the outdoor area.

Area of provision	Enhancements that encourage children to investigate
Water	Place a bucket filled with different sized pebbles next to the water tray and ask the children to, Investigate which pebble makes the greatest splash. Place a bucket of balls which are the same size but made of different materials next to the water tray for the children to, Investigate which balls float or sink.
Sand	Provide a tray of sloppy wet sand, a tray of damp sand and a tray of dry sand and ask the children to, Investigate which sand is the best for building sandcastles.
Construction	Provide a range of construction materials and ask the children to Investigate which are the best materials for building a bridge. Provide margarine cartons, mud, soft clay, wet sand, wet shredded paper and a thick mixture of flour and water and ask the children to, Investigate which material makes the best bricks.
Role Play	Ice cream shack: Use food colouring to colour snow and load it into ice cream containers. Provide scoops and plastic cones. Challenge the children to, Find the best way to stop the 'ice cream' from melting.
Investigation	Set out a selection of objects made of different materials such as metal, plastic, clay and card, together with some magnets. Ask the children to, Investigate which objects are magnetic and challenge them to, Find more magnetic objects around the outdoor area.
Physical	Use playground chalk to draw out a course and place a few cones for weaving around. Provide a three-wheeled scooter, a two-wheeled scooter and a tricycle and invite the children to, Investigate which vehicle is the easiest to navigate around the course.
Garden	Place planters full of flowers in different places around the outdoor area, for instance, shady, spots, sunny spots and in a greenhouse. Help the children care for the flowers with regular watering and weeding. Prompt discussion about the reasons why some flowers are surviving better than others. Ask the children to turn over the soil in the vegetable patch. Provide them with plastic, wooden and metal spades and ask them to, Investigate which are the easiest to dig with.

Curriculum links

Investigating covers the following areas of learning and development:

EYFS	Looks closely at similarities, differences, patterns and change in relation to places, objects, materials and living things; talks about why things happen and how things work (UW).
NIC	Identifies similarities and differences between living things, places, objects and materials; understands that different materials behave in different ways, have different properties and can be used for different purposes; understands that some materials change if kept in different conditions (WAU).
SCE	Develops the skills of scientific inquiry and investigation using practical techniques; investigates the factors affecting plant growth; investigates the effects of friction on motion and explores ways of improving efficiency in moving objects and systems; through creative play, explores different materials and shares reasoning for selecting materials for different purposes (S).
WFPF	Makes comparisons and identifies similarities and differences; sees links between cause and effect; describes what they have found out and offers simple explanations (KUW).

Following instructions

As they progress through their education children will be required to carry out increasingly complex scientific investigations. They will be expected to handle, control and measure variables in order to ensure their tests are fair and systematic. This means they will need to be able to focus and concentrate, as well as listen to and carefully follow instructions. This is also important for safety reasons. Children who are able to concentrate and pay attention are less likely to hurt themselves when handling dangerous equipment and substances.

Following instructions involves the following skills and concepts:

- Being able to focus and concentrate

- Being able to listen attentively

- Being able to maintain two-channeled attention (listen and do)

- Understanding words, phrases and increasingly complex sentences

- Being able to follow and carry out an instruction

- Understanding cause and effect (that doing something may make something else happen).

Children should be given opportunities to develop these fundamental skills for learning from an early age.

The objective of the following activities is to follow instructions carefully to make something happen and it is not necessary to explain the science behind each phenomenon. All of the activities are messy and so best done outside.

Activity 1: Volcanic eruption

Type of activity: Adult-led, small groups.

Resources: Small plastic bottles, self-harding clay or plasticine, red powder paint, warm water, jugs, washing-up liquid, bicarbonate of soda, spoons, vinegar, safety goggles.

What to do: Help the children follow these instructions: Mould clay around the plastic bottle to create the shape of a mountain, taking care to leave the top of the bottle uncovered. Use a jug to pour warm water into the bottle until it is nearly full. Add a squirt of washing-up liquid. Add three heaped spoons of bicarbonate of soda. Pour some vinegar into a jug. Add a spoon of red powder paint and mix well. Pour the vinegar and paint mixture into the volcano and watch it erupt.

Key vocabulary: Volcano, erupt, lava, reaction, vinegar, bicarbonate of soda, listen, follow, instruction, splash, take care.

Assessing and managing risk: Provide safety goggles and ask the children to explain why they may need them.

Teach children to assess and manage risk.

Activity 2: Vegetable soup

Type of activity: Adult-led, small groups.

Resources: Outdoor cooking stove, large cooking pot, wooden spoons, jug, spoons, chopping boards, knives, peelers, two carrots, two parsnips, two potatoes, two leeks, one cabbage, vegetable stock, fresh herbs.

What to do: Help the children follow these instructions: Peel the carrots, parsnips and potatoes and chop them into small pieces. Chop the leeks and cabbage into small pieces. Put the chopped vegetables into a cooking pot. Fill jug with hot tap water. Crumble some vegetable stock cubes into the water and stir until dissolved. Pour the stock into the pot. Chop some fresh herbs and add them too. Bring to the boil and simmer for 20 minutes.

Key vocabulary: Soup, prepare, peel, chop, vegetables, peeler, knife, sharp, cut, cooking pot, stove, hot, burn, stir, mix, flavour, stock, herbs, listen, follow, instruction, glass, take care.

Assessing and managing risk: Children should be closely supervised at all times during this activity. Ensure they are well aware of the dangers of using sharp knives and cooking on a hot stove.

Activity 3: Pin-wheels

Type of activity: Adult-led, small groups.

Resources: Pieces of thin card (15cm x 15cm), scissors, hole punch, sellotape, bendy plastic straws.

What to do: Help the children follow these instructions: Fold the piece of card in half, fold it in half again, then open it back out. Cut about two thirds of the way along each fold, taking care not to cut all the way into the centre of the card. Use a hole punch to punch one hole in each corner of the card, then punch a hole in the centre of the card.

Stick a bendy straw through the hole in the centre. Bring one hole punched corner at a time to the centre, slot it over the straw and stick it down with sellotape. Use scissors to split the straw at the end and bend it back to stop the card coming off. Take the pin-wheels outside and make them spin in the breeze.

Key vocabulary: Pin-wheel, windmill, wind, breeze, spin, turn, round, cut, fold, hole, stick, listen, follow, instruction, scissors, take care.

Assessing and managing risk: Ask the children what they need to do to handle and use scissors safely.

Assessing and managing risk

Involve children in assessing and managing risk. Ask them what they need to be aware of and why they need to take care. Allow them to take controlled risks by handling a variety of materials, substances and resources under close supervision.

Follow instructions to make a dinosaur fossil.

Activity 4: Fossilised

Type of activity: Adult-led, small groups.

Resources: Plaster of Paris (or wall filler), paper bowls, plasticine, dried pasta shapes, teaspoons.

What to do: Help the children follow these instructions: Roll some plasticine into a ball, flatten it and press it into the bottom of a paper bowl. Use pasta shapes to make a picture of a dinosaur by pressing them into the plasticine. Remove the pasta shapes leaving their indentations in the plasticine. Mix some Plaster of Paris in another bowl until smooth. Dollop the plaster on top of the plasticine and smooth it over. Leave it somewhere warm to dry overnight. When the plaster is dry, tear and peel off the paper bowl and remove the plasticine to reveal a fossilised dinosaur skeleton.

Key vocabulary: Fossil, imprint, impression, plasticine, press, Plaster of Paris, mix, pour, set, mould, shape, follow, instruction.

Assessing and managing risk: Ask the children why they should wash their hands thoroughly after handling the Plaster of Paris mix.

Activity 5: Tornado in a jar

Type of activity: Adult-led, small groups.

Resources: Jam jars, water, jugs, food colouring, glitter, washing-up liquid.

What to do: Help the children follow these instructions: Fill a jam jar with water. Add a squirt of washing-up liquid. Add a few drops of food colouring. Add a pinch of glitter. Screw the lid on tight. Swirl the water around in the jar. Watch a mini-tornado appear in the centre.

Key vocabulary: Tornado, water, swirl, twist, vortex, listen, follow, instruction, glass, take care.

Assessing and managing risk: Ask the children why they should handle glass jars with care.

Activity 6: Salt crystals

Type of activity: Adult-led, small groups.

Resources: Epsom salt, measuring jugs, spoons, access to very hot tap water, food colouring, pipettes, clear plastic yogurt lids, safety goggles.

What to do: Help the children to follow these instructions: Use a jug to measure 200ml of Epsom salt and pour it into a bowl. Fill the jug with 200ml of very hot tap water and add a couple of drops of food colouring. Add the coloured water to the salt and stir until the salt is dissolved. Use pipettes squirt just enough of the salty mix to to cover the surface of each clear plastic lid. Leave the lids out in the sunshine for several hours to crystallise. Look closely at the crystal that have formed and compare the different shapes and patterns.

Key vocabulary: Salt, water, measure, mix, warm, dissolve, colour, evaporate, dry, crystal, listen, follow, instruction, hot, splash, take care.

Safety considerations: Ensure the children wear goggles to protect their eyes from the strong salt solution. Warn them to take care when handling hot water.

Pay attention, listen carefully and make things happen.

Enhancing continuous provision

Make pictorial instruction cards that the children can read independently and write lists of instructions that practitioners can read to the children as well. Encourage the children to give instructions, as well as receive them. Provide clipboards, pencils and paper for children to write lists of instructions and draw plans and diagrams for each other to follow.

Area of provision	Enhancements that help children to practise following instructions
Water	Set up an easel next to the water tray with a list of instructions. For example, Float the large blue boat, Sink the small yellow submarine and Find the orange and white striped fish. Encourage the children to give each other similar instructions.
Sand	This is best done in a sand pit but otherwise fill several large trays with sand and place them on the floor. Bury dinosaur bones and fossils in the sand and cordon off the area. Hang a sign saying 'Paleontological sight of special interest'. Provide brushes, small trowels and digital cameras. Make some instruction cards explaining how to excavate a paleontological site. For example, Step 1: Move away the top layer of sand with your hands. Step 2: Use a trowel to carefully uncover the bones. Step 3: Use a brush to sweep away the rest of the sand. Step 4: Take a photo of the bones before removing them from the sand. Put an accompanying photo with each instruction.
Construction	Set out a variety of construction kits with accompanying instruction cards for the children to copy and follow. Provide clipboards, paper and pencils for the children to draw up plans and instructions for each other.
Role Play	Soup kitchen: Fill large cooking pots with water and give the children raw chopped vegetables and fresh herbs to make 'soup'. Provide recipe instruction cards with pictorial measures of ingredients along with cups, spoons and jugs to measure with.
Investigation	Provide a small treasure chest and challenge the children to hide it and either give verbal instructions or draw an instructional diagram or map to guide others to find it.
Physical	Provide playground chalks, cones and blindfolds for the children to draw out a course, then blindfold and lead each other through it using verbal instructions. Sit a puppet in a large space next to a sign inviting children to come and play Simon Says. Model using the puppet to start a game then hand the puppet over to the children so they can practise calling out the instructions. Gather children together to play parachute games and invite volunteers to call out the instructions.
Garden	Make growing instruction cards. For example, Step 1: Choose a plant pot. Step 2: Fill it with soil. Step 3: Make a hole, drop in a seed and cover it over. Step 4: Water the seed. Step 5: Place the pot in a warm sunny spot. Display the cards in a gardening shed or on the inside of windows facing out.

Curriculum links

Following instructions covers the following areas of learning and development:

EYFS	Follows instructions involving several ideas or actions; maintains attention and concentrates; understands more complex sentences; develops understanding of simple concepts; understands use of objects; follows instructions involving several ideas or actions; uses talk to organise, sequence and clarify thinking (CL). Shows understanding of the need for safety when tackling new challenges, and considers and manages some risks (PD).
NIC	Explores how to keep safe (PDMU). Listens to and carries out increasingly complex instructions; listens with increasing attentiveness for longer periods of time; takes part and contributes to group oral language activities; talks about work, play and things they have made (LL).
SCE	Applies safety measures and takes necessary actions to control risk and hazards (S). When talking in different situations is learning to take turns and is developing an awareness of when to talk and when to listen; listens or watches for useful or interesting information and uses this to make choices or learn new things; shares ideas and information in a way that communicates their messages (LE).
WFPF	Becomes more aware of personal safety; concentrates for lengthening periods (PSD). Listens and responds appropriately and effectively, with growing attention and concentration; listens to and carries out instructions; talks/communicates, spontaneously and through structured activities, for a variety of purposes (LLC).

Measuring

Scientific investigation involves measuring in order to identify difference and change, make comparisons and find links and explanations. In the early years children need to form an understanding of what measurement is and why it is important. This means setting up meaningful experiences that demonstrate the purpose of measurement before going on use standard measuring equipment.

Measuring involves the following skills and concepts:

- Being able to make comparisons and identify similarities and differences

- Understanding cause and effect (that changing something may have an affect on something else)

- Being able to describe measurements in non-standard terms such as 'full', 'empty', 'close', 'far', 'tall', 'short', 'high', 'low', 'heavy', 'light', 'fast', 'slow', 'loud', 'quiet', 'hot' and 'cold'

- Understanding the need to take measurements

- Recognising and using standard units of measurement such as 'centimetre', 'metre', 'gram', 'kilogram', 'second', 'minute', 'litre', 'pint' and 'degrees centigrade'.

Introduce younger children to measurements by planning experiences that prompt them to make simple comparisons that do not yet involve taking accurate measurements. For example, comparing temperatures in terms of cold, warm and hot, distances in terms of close and far away and capacity in terms of full and empty. Once they understand these basic concepts move on to using measuring equipment and introduce units of measure.

Activity 1: By bus or on foot

Type of activity: Adult-led, small groups.

Resources: Watch, enough adults for an off-site trip.

What to do: Compare how long it takes to get somewhere by bus compared to walking. Leave on foot, checking the time on the way out. When you arrive check the time again and tell the children how long it took. Return by bus, again checking the time on departure and arrival. Compare which journey took the longest and talk about why.

Make it purposeful: Involve the children in making decisions about how to travel to places off-site. Talk about how far away the destination is and how long it will take by foot or bus/coach.

Key vocabulary: Journey, travel, distance, how far? time, quick, slow, quickest, slowest, walk, bus, vehicle.

Extension ideas: Help the children to consider the impact that science has had on our lives with the invention of motorised transport. Use information books to find out how difficult life is for people in other parts of the world who cannot afford vehicles or do not have the same infrastructure to allow ease of travel.

Find out how long it takes to walk somewhere.

Activity 3: Windsocks

Type of activity: Adult-led, small groups.

Resources: Shredded plastic bags, large plastic lemonade bottles, scissors, string.

What to do: Cut up some plastic lemonade bottles into wide plastic hoops. Help the children tie shredded strips of plastic bag around each hoop (take care in case the bottle edges are sharp). Tie each end of a piece of string to either side of the hoop and hang the windsock outside. Observe the windsock in various weathers and talk about and describe the strength and direction of the wind.

Make it purposeful: Use the windsocks to help decide when it is a good day to go kite flying.

Key vocabulary: Windsock, wind, breeze, gale, strong, light, weak, blowing, gust, direction.

Extension ideas: Draw a compass on the floor near a windsock so the children can see which direction the wind is blowing. Make small hand-held windsocks that the children can take outside and run around with.

Activity 2: Ramp it up

Type of activity: Adult-led, small groups.

Resources: Crates or blocks, sheet of wood or plastic, different coloured small toy vehicles, playground chalks, measuring tape.

What to do: Build a ramp and set out some small vehicles next to it. Bring some children over and explain you would like to find out which vehicle will travel the furthest when rolled down the ramp. Roll one vehicle down the ramp and mark where it stops with a matching coloured chalk. Move the vehicle out of the way and repeat with the other vehicles. Look at the chalk marks and ask the children to identify which vehicle travelled the furthest. Introduce a measuring tape to measure the actual distance each vehicle travelled.

Key vocabulary: Ramp, slope, travel, down, how far? furthest, wheels, fast, slow, distance, stop, go, roll, measure, centimetre, metre.

Make it purposeful: Give the children a reason to measure how far the different cars travel by drawing a race track with finishing line at the base of the ramp. This turns the activity into a game that will encourage the children to choose vehicles that are most likely to reach the finish.

Extension ideas: Challenge the children to make the vehicles travel further by altering the gradient of the ramp to make it more or less steep. Measure how high each ramp is, using non-standard units (crates/blocks) and standard units (cm).

Go sledging to learn about speed and distance.

Activity 4: Rain gauge

Type of activity: Adult-initiated, during independent play.

Resources: Large plastic bottle, sharp scissors, permanent marker, ruler, wire.

What to do: Make a rain gauge and leave it outside to collect rainwater. Cut the top off a plastic bottle, turn it upside down and put it back on so it acts like a funnel. Use a ruler and permanent marker to draw a measuring scale on the side of the bottle. Put the bottle outside in the open and secure it to something like a railing using a piece of wire.

After a week invite some children over to the bottle and look at how much water is inside. Check if the children can say where the water has come from. Help them read the measuring scale to find out how many centimetres of rain there has been in the last week.

Make it purposeful: Use the rain gauge to keep track of how much rain has fallen when deciding how much to water outdoor plants.

Key vocabulary: Rainfall, water, rain gauge, measure, centimetre.

Extension ideas: Make a chart to record the rainfall over several weeks.

Activity 5: Sledging

Type of activity: Adult-led, small groups.

Resources: Sloped area suitable and safe for sledging, enough adults for an off-site trip, sledges, warm waterproof clothing.

What to do: Take small groups of children sledging in snowy weather. Choose a place where the terrain has slopes of different gradients, some steeper than others. Invite the children to have a go at sledging down the different slopes. Point out how far the sledges go on the steeper slopes. Find out if sledges carrying adults travel further than those carrying children. Talk about why sledges with a heavier load travel further than those with lighter loads. Compare the speeds of the sledges carrying adults and children. Which go faster and why? Help the children consider how this relates to the distance the sledges travel.

Make it purposeful: Have a sledging competition to see who can travel the furthest.

Key vocabulary: Sledge, snow, glide, travel, further, slow, fast, steep, gentle, slope, hill, smooth, distance, stop, start, heavy, light.

Extension ideas: Use a measuring tape and measure the sledge tracks to find out how far they travelled.

Make your own rain gauge to measure rainfall.

Try…

…planning activities that prompt children to compare measures in relation to cause and effect, for instance, why one vehicle travels faster than another, why one load is more difficult to move than another and why ear defenders block out more sound than earmuffs.

Enhancing continuous provision

The following suggestions are for activities and resources that will encourage children to play with measuring. For each area of provision there are both ideas for activities that involve non-standard units of measure as well as resources that will help children become familiar with standard units.

Area of provision	Enhancements that encourage children to measure
Water	Non-standard: Fill buckets with cold, tepid and warm water for the children to compare temperatures. Non-standard: Provide different sized and shaped jugs, bottles, buckets, spoons and ladles. Standard: Provide different sized scaled measuring jugs, cylinders, beakers and medicine syringes.
Sand	Non-standard: Make a monster truck obstacle course and provide radio controlled vehicles for the children to compare speeds as they travel up and over the obstacles. Standard: Provide small plastic bottles with holes punched in the lids and masking tape for the children to make sand timers using very dry sand. Give the children digital timers to time the sand as it pours through and find out the durations of their timers.
Construction	Non-standard: Set up a pulley system and provide wheelbarrows and trolleys. Provide a wide range of bricks, stones and rocks for the children to compare the amount of force needed to transport and move different weights. Standard: Provide scales for children to weigh and compare wooden, foam and cork bricks.
Role Play	Emergency ambulance: Use a large cardboard box to make an ambulance. Supply uniforms and put together a paramedic kit full of toy medical equipment, including a blood pressure and heart monitor. Provide real measuring equipment such as weighing scales, forehead thermometers, a height chart and nurses' watches.
Investigation	Non-standard: Provide musical instruments along with ear muffs and ear defenders for the children to partially and wholly block out sound and compare the difference. Standard: Make sundials. (Find printable templates on the Royal Museums Greenwich website: www.nmm.ac.uk/make-your-own/sundial)
Physical	Non-standard: Set out tunnels in different sizes and lengths for children to crawl through and different sized cardboard boxes for them to climb inside. Standard: Set up a race track and provide stopwatches for the children to time how long it takes to run/skip/walk/jump to the finish line.
Garden	Non-standard: Set up a battery powered train with fast and slow settings for the children to alter speed. Non-standard: Draw around puddles with chalk. Revisit them every hour throughout the day to draw around them again as they evaporate and reduce in size. Standard: Put a weatherproof thermometer outside and another inside a greenhouse or indoor growing area. Help the children read and compare the temperatures.

Curriculum links

Measuring covers the following areas of learning and development:

EYFS	Talks about why things happen and how things work (UW). Uses everyday language to talk about time, capacity, weight, length and height; measures short periods of time in simple ways; orders items by capacity, weight, length and height (M).
NIC	Asks questions and talks about why things happen (WAU). Talks about observations in terms of took longer/shorter time; compares objects of different capacity, weight, length and height; chooses and uses, with guidance, non-standard units to measure time, capacity, weight, length and height (MN).
SCE	Develops the skills of scientific inquiry and investigation using practical techniques; recognises the impact the sciences make on their lives and the lives of others (S). Experiments with everyday items as units of measure to investigate and compare sizes and amounts in the environment, sharing findings with others (NMM).
WFPF	Makes observations and measurements (KUW). Compares and orders objects in terms of capacity, volume, mass, length and height; uses non-standard units for comparison, and sees the need for standard units of measure; chooses units and measuring equipment appropriate to the relevant measuring task; reads a scale with some accuracy (MD).

Hypothesising

Another aspect of investigating is hypothesising, or trying to explain why something might be happening. Hypothesis involves examining and weighing up information and using it to inform thinking and reasoning.

Therefore, young children's ability to hypothesise depends on whether they are able to process information, make connections and explain their logic. Being able to hypothesise is an important first step towards making predictions.

Making a hypothesis involves the following skills and concepts:

- Being able to make comparisons and identify similarities and differences

- Understanding cause and effect (that changing something may have an affect on something else)

- Being able to draw upon knowledge and experience to offer an explanation

- Being able to find links between different pieces of information and connect ideas

- Being able to verbally express ideas and explain reasoning.

Children who are given plenty of time to explore a variety of scientific phenomena will have a greater understanding of how the world works. It is, therefore, important to plan experiences that involve observing, examining and manipulating a wide range of objects, materials and living things in different situations and under a variety of conditions to find out how they behave. This aspect of science is closely related to communication and language and practitioners can help by encouraging children to describe what they see and share their thinking.

Activity 1: Pooh Sticks

Type of activity: Adult-led, small groups.

Resources: Low bridge over moving water, different sized and shaped sticks.

What to do: This activity is best done in a wooded area with a nearby stream and low bridge. Help the children to collect some sticks then take them to a low bridge that is safe to stand on while dropping things off the side. Invite a child to choose a stick and drop it into the water. Together watch the stick travel under the bridge and come out the other side. Invite another child to choose a different sized stick and drop it in. Ask the children to describe what happens. Does the stick travel faster or slower? Does it float or sink? Does it get stuck on anything? Can the children explain why?

Allow the children to experiment with dropping different sized and shaped sticks into the water. Encourage them to discuss what happens with each.

Key vocabulary: Stick, float, water, moving, upstream, downstream, stuck, faster, slower, smaller, bigger, shape, why?

Extension ideas: Try dropping the sticks in different parts of the water. Try dropping them off the other side of the bridge to see what happens.

Take a visit to a local river or stream and have a game of Pooh Sticks.

Activity 2: Submarines

Type of activity: Adult-led, small groups.

Resources: Equal sized plastic bottles, bendy drinking straws, deep water tray.

What to do: Place the bottles on top of the water in the tray so that they are floating. Invite the children to pick the bottles up, look inside then push them under the water. Encourage the children to explain what is happening as the bottles fill with water and sink below the surface.

Give each child a drinking straw and ask them to feed one end into the neck of a bottle and blow into the other end.

Watch as the bottles begin to float back up to the surface. Can the children explain what is happening? (They are blowing light air into the bottles, which is pushing the heavy water out so the bottles are becoming lighter and floating back up to the surface.)

Key vocabulary: Empty, water, fill, full, air, light, heavy, sink, float.

Extension ideas: Experiment with filling some of the bottles with pieces of sponge and large marbles before trying to blow air in again. Can the children suggest why it is not working this time?

Activity 3: Yucky slides

Type of activity: Adult-initiated, during independent play.

Resources: Plastic trays or sheets of wood covered in plastic sheeting, shaving foam, water, jelly, washing-up liquid, cooking oil, honey, small wooden bricks, containers.

What to do: Prop up a series of plastic trays so they are sloped like slides. Cover each tray in a different substance, for example, shaving foam, water, mushed up jelly, washing-up liquid, honey and cooking oil. Place a tub of small wooden cubes next to each slide. Invite the children to place the bricks at the top of the trays and watch them slide down. Encourage them to talk about what is happening. Can they explain why some bricks are sliding quicker than others? Get the children to rub the substances in their hands and describe what they feel like.

Key vocabulary: Slide, down, fast, slow, slippery, smooth, runny, slimy, sticky, friction, affect/effect, why?

Extension ideas: Set the slides at different gradients.

Build a waterway and investigate how water behaves.

Activity 4: Mini paratroopers

Type of activity: Adult-led, small groups.

Resources: Thin plastic bag (bin liners are good), tissue paper, thin card, greaseproof paper, netting, tarpaulin, ruler, scissors, cotton thread, hole punch, toy figurines

What to do: Cut out a square of thin plastic approximately 30cm x 30cm and punch a hole in each corner. Cut four 30cm lengths of cotton thread and tie each to a corner of the plastic. Tie the other ends of the thread to a toy person. Make more of the same sized parachutes out of different materials.

Take the children somewhere where they can stand safely and drop the parachutes from up high, for example, behind the railing at the top of a footbridge or flight of stairs. Invite a child to drop the thin plastic parachute and watch it fall. Encourage the children to describe what happened, how the parachute behaved and why. Repeat with the other parachutes.

Key vocabulary: Fast, slow, glide, fall, drop, down, crash, float, material, different, affect/effect, why?

Extension ideas: Test different sized parachutes made out of the same material. Try paper parachutes that are flat, folded or scrunched up.

Activity 5: Waterway

Type of activity: Adult-initiated, during independent play.

Resources: Hurdle stands, crates and blocks, various lengths of guttering and pipes, jugs, buckets.

What to do: Set up a water way by resting lengths of guttering and pipes on hurdle stands, crates and blocks. Arrange them so they are sloped in different directions and on various gradients. Include at least one that is lying level. Fill buckets with water and provide jugs for the children to pour it onto the pipes and guttering. Encourage the children to observe which way the water is flowing. Is the water collecting anywhere? Is it leaking or overflowing at any point? Why? Does the water travel up slopes? Can the children explain why the water is behaving the way it is?

Key vocabulary: Water, guttering, pipes, pour, flow, leak, overflow, running, uphill, downhill, across, through.

Extension ideas: Take the waterway apart and challenge the children to build a new one that will transport water from one particular place to another.

Don't forget to think about…

…planning more complex investigations to challenge more able children. Each time children's preconceptions are challenged they have to accommodate new ideas, helping them to move on in their learning. Set up investigations that challenge the children's thinking by showing unexpected results and surprises.

Find out what material makes the best parachute.

Enhancing continuous provision

Set up activities and provocations that grab children's attention and get them hypothesising about how and why things are happening. Leave things out for them to discover and wonder about. As the children play and explore engage them in conversation and encourage them to describe what they can see and what is going on. Ask them to offer explanations as to why. It does not matter if the children are unable to come up with accurate explanations. Hypothesising is about coming up with ideas. Challenge misconceptions and see if they can come up with alternative theories. Use questions such as 'why do you think that?', 'how do you know that?' and 'how can we find out?' to get the children making connections, explaining their reasoning and testing their ideas.

Area of provision	Enhancements that encourage children to hypothesise
Water	Half fill some large plastic transparent containers with water beads. Pour water onto the beads, seal the containers and leave them outside where the children can see them. Throughout the day watch as the beads expand and the water disappears. Once they have fully absorbed the water tip the beads into a water tray for the children to examine. Ask the children if they can explain what has happened.
Sand	Collect several cups of sand and dye them different colours by damping the sand with water and adding food colouring or fabric dye. Dry the sand and use it to create a picture in a shallow tray or tuff spot. Leave it for the children to discover and ask them if they can explain where the sand came from and how it has been coloured.
Construction	Provide cardboard construction materials including food packaging, tubes and different sized pieces of card, and some masking tape. Challenge the children to make a bridge that they can drive toy vehicles across. Can they explain what it is about cardboard that makes the task easy/difficult?
Role Play	Bird hide: Use a tent or very large cardboard box covered in camouflage netting to make a bird hide. Hang bird feeders in different places all over the outdoor area; high up, low down, in quiet and noisy areas, in the sun and shade. Ask the children if they can explain why the birds visit some feeders more than others.
Investigation	Make a polycup telephone: Use two polystyrene cups. Pierce a hole in the centre of the base of each and thread through and knot the ends of a three-metre length of string. Invite the children to try out the telephone and ask if they can explain how it works.
Physical	Set out a range of balancing equipment such as benches, balance boards, stepping stones and stilts for the children to use. Ask them if they can explain why it is difficult to balance on the different pieces of equipment.
Garden	Make sun catchers using old CDs and coloured glass beads threaded onto catgut. Hang them all over the garden area, some in direct sunlight and others in the shade. Ask the children if they can explain why some are sparkling and others are not. Give them white paper to catch the coloured rays of light and ask if they can explain what is happening.

Curriculum links

Hypothesising covers the following areas of learning and development:

EYFS	Talks about why things happen and how things work; makes observations of objects, materials and living things and explains why some things occur, and talks about changes (UW). Uses talk to connect ideas and explain what is happening (CL).
NIC	Asks questions and talks about why things happen (WAU). Asks questions, describes and explains; answers questions to give information and demonstrate understanding; offers reasons to support opinions given (LL).
SCE	Investigates the factors affecting plant growth; investigates the effects of friction on motion and explores ways of improving efficiency in moving objects and systems; explores different materials and shares reasoning for selecting materials for different purposes (S). Asks questions and links learning with what they already know; shares experiences and feelings, ideas and information in a way that communicates their messages (LE).
WFPF	Sees links between cause and effect; recognises simple patterns in their findings; describes what they have found out and offers simple explanations (KUW). Talks/communicates, spontaneously and through structured activities, for a variety of purposes, expressing thoughts and ideas (LLC).

Predicting

Young children's ability to make accurate predictions is dependent upon their prior experience and ability to hypothesise. This means children should have opportunities to observe and explore a wide range of objects, materials and living things.

Again there is a need for good communication and language skills as children are required to recall past experiences, make connections and explain their ideas and reasoning.

Making a prediction involves the following skills and concepts:

- Understanding cause and effect (that changing something may have an affect on something else)

- Being able to find links between different pieces of information and connect ideas

- Being able to hypothesise (explain why something might be happening)

- Being able to draw upon knowledge and experience to make an informed guess

- Being able to verbally express thoughts and explain reasoning.

In the early years children need plenty of practice doing simple investigations where they are engaged in sustained shared thinking and encouraged to hypothesise and make predictions about what will happen next. This experience will increase their knowledge and understanding of the world and lead to their making ever more accurate predictions, which will prepare them for more complex and challenging investigations later on. Following are some simple investigations that encourage children to make a prediction.

Activity 1: What will they do?

Type of activity: Adult-led, small groups.

Prior experience needed: Children need to have had experience of observing different minibeasts in various habitats. They should have also read information books to find out about how they live and behave.

Resources: Magnifiers.

What to do: Take the children out hunting for minibeasts and see if they can use their knowledge to predict behaviours. For example:

Worms: Gently remove a worm from the soil and place it on your hand. Watch it for a while and encourage the children to share what they know about worms. Ask them to predict what will happen when you place the worm back on top of the soil. Where will it go? Why?

Spiders: Find a spider sitting in the centre of a web. Watch it and ask the children to share what they know about spiders. Ask the children to predict what might happen if you gently touch one of the threads on the web. What might the spider do? Why?

Woodlice: Look under logs and rocks for woodlice. Again, watch the woodlice and encourage the children to tell you what they know about them. Ask the children to predict what will happen if you roll a log over and leave it upturned. What will the woodlice do? Where will they go? Why?

Key vocabulary: Minibeast, spider, worm, woodlice, live, move, soil, damp, home, web, habitat, happy, unhappy, safe, what would happen if…? why?

Extension ideas: Try asking the children hypothetical questions about minibeasts that are not present. For example; What might a wasp do if you swat it? What would happen to a snail if it sat in the sun for too long?

What would happen if a snail sat out in the sun for too long?

Activity 2: Painting on snow

Type of activity: Adult-initiated, during independent play.

Prior experience needed: Children need to have had experience of playing with snow, picking it up in their hands and watching it melt.

Resources: Squeezy bottles (washing-up, shampoo, shower gel), poster paints.

What to do: Fill some squeezy bottles with water and add a little paint to each bottle. Give them a shake to make a watery paint mixture. Show the bottles to the children and ask them what they think would happen if they were to squirt the paint onto snow. Give out the bottles and allow the children time and space to have a go at creating some pictures and patterns.

When the children are finished ask them what they think is going to happen to the pictures they have created when the snow melts. Do they think the pictures will disappear? What will happen to the paint? Return to the site when the snow has melted and see what has happened.

Key vocabulary: Snow, paint, water, melt, disappear, remain, pattern, colour, squeeze, squirt, what will happen?

Extension ideas: Provide warm and cold paint mixes for the children to use and see what happens.

What will happen to the paint when the snow melts?

How many weights will it take to crack the ice?

Activity 4: Hard as rock

Type of activity: Adult-led, small groups.

Prior experience needed: Children need to have had experience of handling and playing with small, large, thick and thin pieces of ice. They should have had a chance to freeze water to make ice, watched ice melt and had a go at breaking ice.

Resources: Plastic containers, standard weights or different sized stones, crates or wooden blocks.

What to do: Freeze some relatively large blocks of ice in varying thicknesses. Place two crates next to each other leaving a gap in between and place a thick piece of ice and a thin piece next to each other bridging the gap. Pass some weights around for the children to feel. Ask them what they think might happen if they put the weights on the thick piece of ice then invite them to place some weights on it. Ask them to consider what might happen if they put the same amount of weight on the thinner piece. Encourage them to explain the reasons behind their thinking. Invite them to put some weights on the thinner piece and watch what happens. Continue to experiment with placing weights on different thicknesses of ice.

Key vocabulary: Ice, hard, frozen, compact, solid, thick, strong, thin, brittle, weak, heavy, weight, break, why?

Extension ideas: If you have snow, pick pieces of frozen snow from the ground and test it against the solid ice. Can the children predict whether it will be able to hold the weights? Once they have tested it, can they explain why not?

Activity 3: Soak it up

Type of activity: Adult-led, small groups.

Prior experience needed: Children need to have experience of playing with water, pouring it into containers, moving it around, spilling it on the floor, mopping it up, sweeping it, splashing in it and getting themselves wet.

Resources: Empty water tray, jug of water, sponge.

What to do: Pass the sponge around for the children to feel and squeeze. Pour a small amount of water into a water tray and ask the children to predict what will happen if you put the sponge in the water. Drop the sponge in the tray and watch it absorb the water.

Lift the sponge out of the tray and pass it around the children. Ask them to tell you how it feels now. Can they explain why? Invite a child to squeeze the sponge over the water tray so the children can observe the water coming back out. Again, encourage them to explain what is happening.

Key vocabulary: Sponge, water, soak, absorb, dry, wet, heavy, squeeze out, what if...? why?

Extension ideas: Use pipettes to squirt coloured water onto pale sponges so the children can observe absorption happening.

What might happen if you mix mud with sand?

Enhancing continuous provision

Encourage children to make predictions by setting up activities that get them thinking about What might happen if…?

Joining their play and ask questions such as, 'what might happen if we add water to the sand?' or 'what might happen if we use smaller bricks to build the tower?' Get them used to drawing on their prior knowledge and experience, for

example, by getting them to make comparisons between objects and materials, considering their properties and predicting which is most suitable for a particular task. Ask the children if they have ever seen anything like this before and prompt them to think about what happened last time before guessing what will happen in this particular situation.

Following are some ideas for provocations and activities that aim to get children making predictions as they play.

Area of provision	Enhancements that encourage children to make predictions
Water	Build two waterways next to each other and ask the children if they can predict which the water will travel down the fastest. Fill a tub with a variety of everyday objects and ask the children to predict which will float or sink.
Sand	Create a large picture on the floor using dry coloured sand. Provide watering cans with sprinkler attachments and small buckets filled with water. Ask the children to predict what will happen to the picture if they pour, sprinkle or drench it with water. Allow them to have a go and see what happens.
Construction	Build a series of tall towers with different types of bricks including small wooden cubes, interlocking bricks and large wooden blocks. Provide a bucket of medium sized firm balls and ask the children to predict what will happen if they roll the balls at the base of each tower. Will the tower topple? Why/why not? How will it fall? How can they prevent it from falling?
Role Play	Mud pie kitchen: Provide bowls of sand, soft clay, flour and water. Ask the children to predict what will happen if they mix these into mud. What will happen to the consistency of the mud? What will it look like? Ask the children to predict what will happen if they leave their mud pies out in the rain or sun.
Investigation	Cut some thin slices of fruit and vegetables, put them out in the sun and ask the children to predict what will happen to them. Wedge a broom handle in a bucket full of sand and stand it in the sun. Use playground chalk and draw a line along the shadow of the handle. Ask the children to predict what will happen to the shadow as the day goes on. Blow up some balloons. Do not tie them, just hold them at the neck and ask the children to predict what will happen if you let them go.
Physical	Set up some skittles and provide different types of balls such as sponge, ping-pong, inflatable and footballs. Ask the children to predict which ball will knock down the most skittles. Fill a tub with different balls and ask the children to predict which will bounce the highest. Provide beanbags, large balls and small wooden blocks and ask the children to predict which will be the easiest to balance on their head whilst walking from A to B.
Garden	Sew cress seeds in shallow containers and put them in different places around the outdoor area. Ask the children to predict which seeds will germinate and grow the quickest. Collect some minibeasts and place them bug viewing containers. Ask the children to predict what would happen if you kept the minibeasts in these small containers and did not release them. (Remember minibeasts should be released from bug viewers within 30 minutes.)

Curriculum links

Making predictions covers the following areas of learning and development:

EYFS	Uses talk to connect ideas, explain what is happening and anticipate what might happen next; uses talk to recall and relive past experiences (CL).
NIC	Talks about experiences, recalls, predicts, explains; answers questions to give information and demonstrate understanding; offers reasons to support opinions given (LL).
SCE	Asks questions and links learning with what they already know; shares experiences and feelings, ideas and information in a way that communicates their messages (LE).
WFPF	Sees links between cause and effect; thinks about what might happen if…; participates in play and planned activities that build on previous experiences; recognises simple patterns in their findings (KUW).

Coming up with ideas

Part of science education is helping children to appreciate scientific endeavour and human achievement in terms of the 'big ideas' that have transformed the world. Such ideas are born from inventive minds and it is therefore important that we foster creative thinking in young people so they develop the imagination needed to become the scientists of the future.

Coming up with ideas involves the following skills:

- Being curious about the features of the natural and man-made environment

- Being able to find links between different pieces of information and connect ideas

- Being open to new ideas and able to take on the ideas of others

- Being able to come up with original ideas and find new ways to do things

- Being able to plan, make decisions and select appropriate resources to accomplish a task

- Being able to verbally express ideas and explain reasoning.

Helping children to become creative thinkers means encouraging them to think for themselves. Present children with provocations that introduce some of the 'big ideas' of science and use these as a springboard for encouraging them to use their imaginations and come up with inventions of their own. Where better to start than with some of the greatest scientific discoveries that were either made or developed outdoors?

Activity 1: Shift it

Type of activity: Adult-initiated, during independent play.

Resources: Wide plank of wood, several cylindrical pieces of wood.

What to do: Begin by showing children photographs of the ancient Egyptian pyramids and explaining they were built before cars, lorries and cranes existed. Explain you are going to show them some ways of moving heavy objects without machines or vehicles.

Transporting: Lay a wide plank of wood on several rollers. Choose a child and help them sit on top of the plank. Invite the other children to gently push the plank forwards (taking care not to trap fingers) until one roller is exposed at the back. Ask the children to lift the roller, carry it around and place it at the front. Push the plank forwards again and repeat with the next roller. Continue until the child has been moved to the other side of the space.

Lifting: Set up a pulley system by looping a piece of rope over the side of a climbing frame. Ask a child to climb up the frame and hold one end of the rope. Then tie the other end to a large bucket on the ground. Fill the bucket with stones or sand. Ask some other children to have a go at lifting it, taking care not to strain their backs. Note how difficult this is then ask the child with the rope to give it a pull and see if this is any easier.

Key vocabulary: Move, transport, lift, weight, heavy, pulley, roller, push, pull, easier, more difficult.

Help the children take it further: Provide pipes and trays for children to make their own roller transportation. Provide rope and buckets for them to make their own pulleys.

Experiment with different ways of moving heavy loads.

Activity 2: What goes up must come down

Type of activity: Adult-initiated, during independent play.

Resources: Globe, range of balls.

What to do: Show the children a globe and explain that everything stays on planet Earth because of a force called gravity. Gravity stops everything floating away by pulling it to earth. That is why every time we throw a ball into the air it drops back down to the ground. Give the children a range of heavy and light balls to take outside, throw in the air and watch fall to the ground. Can they make their ball stay in the air?

Take the children to a gentle slope and ask what they think will happen if they lie down at the top tip and roll themselves over the side. Allow the children to have a go. When they are at the bottom challenge them to roll back up again. Can they explain why they cannot do this without grabbing onto the grass and pulling themselves up? Gravity is working against them. They are being pulled downward as they try to roll uphill.

Key vocabulary: Gravity, up, down, fall, drop, pull, throw.

Help the children take it further: Provide a marble run kit for the children to construct and play with. Provide cardboard tubes and masking tape for them to build their own. Set out guttering and pipes to make ramps and shoots to roll balls, vehicles and water down.

Roll down a hill, then try to roll back up again.

Find out why some paper aeroplanes fly better than others.

Activity 4: Taking flight

Type of activity: Adult-led, during independent play.

Resources: Pictures of aircraft, A4 paper, aeroplane designs find a selection with video tutorials on Australian website (www.kidspot.com.au/kids-activities-and-games/Activity-ideas+30/10-of-the-best-paper-plane-designs+12392.htm).

What to do: Show the children pictures of aircraft from over the past 100 years since the aeroplane was first invented. Go outside and watch for aeroplanes passing overhead. Ask if any of the children have ever been on a plane. Explain why they are such a significant invention and how they have changed the world.

Help the children use A4 paper to make a variety of paper aeroplane designs. Take the aeroplanes outside on a calm dry day and test the different designs to find out which fly the best. Ask the children to describe how the different planes move and how far they go. Can the children offer any explanations as to why some aeroplanes fly better than others? Give them time to play with, compare and discuss the different designs and experiment with different ways of throwing them.

Key vocabulary: Aeroplane, flight, fly, travel, sky, air, distance, design, throw, better, worse, how far? furthest, affect/effect, why?

Help the children take it further: Display posters of aircraft on the inside of windows facing out. Provide different types of paper for the children to make more aeroplanes. Give them toy polystyrene gliders and Balsa wood aeroplane kits to build and test.

Activity 3: Wind power

Type of activity: Adult-led, small groups.

Resources: Construction kits for building small vehicles, thin dowel rod, plasticine, thin card, small hand-held fans.

What to do: Explain how it is possible to harness and use the force of the wind to power machines. Show the children a clip of some people kite buggying on the BBC Bitesize website (www.bbc.co.uk/education/clips/zqd9wmn). Explain the children are going to make small wind powered vehicles of their own.

Provide construction materials and ask the children to make a vehicle chassis (a base with four wheels). Give each child a 10cm x 20cm piece of thin card and a 20cm length of thin dowel rod. Help the children push the end of their doweling rods through the top centre of their pieces of card and again through the bottom centre to create curved sails. Give each child a ball of plasticine so they can stick their sails to the vehicle chassis they have built.

Take the cars outside and play with them in the wind. Can the children think of ways to channel the wind so it catches the sails? (If there is no wind use small hand-held fans to generate a breeze to push them along.)

Key vocabulary: Wind, power, energy, force, push, move, sail, catch, vehicle.

Help the children take it further: Display posters of wind powered machines such as windmills and sail boats on the inside of windows facing out. Place windmills and flags around the outdoor area for the children to observe. Provide materials for the children to experiment with making their own kites, windmills and flags.

Introduce children to some of science's 'big ideas'.

Enhancing continuous provision

Provide toys and equipment that will enable children to explore a range of scientific inventions and discoveries. Provide a range of resources that will inspire them to create inventions of their own.

Display pictures depicting some of the 'big ideas' of science. Hang laminated photo books on easels and display pictures in sheds or inside windows facing out. Lay out a picnic blanket and provide information books for the children to find out more.

Area of provision	Enhancements that showcase 'big ideas' and encourage children to come up with ideas of their own
Water	Display pictures of boats and ships near the water tray. Provide books about sea transport. Provide water wheels, wind-up propeller powered toys and sail boats. Supply a box filled with plastic tubs, straws, lolly sticks and short lengths of dowel rod.
Sand	Display pictures of builders mixing and using cement with up-close images of bricks cemented together. Provide information books about construction. Provide bricks along with sand, cement powder and water for the children to mix and build with. (Ensure this is closely supervised and give the children face masks, goggles and gloves to wear.)
Construction	Provide construction kits that encourage children to invent and design, hollow building blocks, Sticklebricks, nuts and bolts, interlocking tubes, gears and cogs, LEGO, Magnetico and Mobilo.
Role Play	Space shuttle: Stick silver stars onto a black sheet of fabric and drape it over some chairs. Make a control panel by painting cardboard boxes silver, drawing on number pads and controls with permanent marker and sticking on colourful stickers. Provide information books about space travel and living in space for children to refer to and further develop the area themselves.
Investigation	Challenge the children to source items from around the outdoor area to make musical instruments. Give the children a range of battery operated toys to play with. Build a den using blackout material and provide torches to use inside.
Physical	Display pictures of children using aides designed to help them overcome physical disability, for example, wheelchairs, mobility scooters, stair-lifts, hearing aids and guide dogs. Provide storybooks such as *It's Okay to be Different* by Todd Parr and *Don't Call Me Special* by Pat Thomas.
Garden	Display pictures industrial sized greenhouses and working tractors. Provide information books about the machinery and technology used in farming and agriculture. Place solar powered lights around the garden area. Set up a miniature greenhouse next to an outdoor growing area.

Curriculum links

Coming up with ideas covers the following areas of learning and development:

EYFS	Talks about why things happen and how things work; recognises that a range of technology is used in places such as homes and schools (UW). Will talk about their ideas and choose the resources needed for chosen activities (PSED). Uses talk to organise and clarify thinking and ideas; listens and responds to ideas expressed by others (CL). Uses what they have learnt about media and materials in original ways, thinking about uses and purposes (EAD).
NIC	Asks questions and talks about why things happen; is aware of everyday uses of technological tools (WAU). Shows a positive attitude towards learning; shows independence and knows when to seek help (PDMU). Talks about their work and things they have made; shares thoughts and ideas with different audiences (LL). Uses direct experiences, memory and imagination to observe and respond to the world (AD).
SCE	Recognises the impact the sciences make on their lives and the lives of others (S). Has the freedom to discover and choose ways to create using a variety of materials; uses curiosity and imagination to solve design problems (AD). In everyday activity and play, explores and makes choices to develop learning and interests (HW). Shares experiences, ideas and information in a way that communicates their message (LE).
WFPF	Thinks creatively and imaginatively; becomes aware of human achievements and the 'big ideas' that have shaped the world (KUW). Becomes an independent thinker and learner; responds to ideas and questions enthusiastically, sensitively, creatively, and intuitively; expresses ideas and feelings creatively, explaining why they are significant (PSD). Talks/communicates, spontaneously and through structured activities, for a variety of purposes, expressing thoughts, ideas and needs (LLC).

Problem solving

Science is about looking for inventive ways to solve problems. Scientists ask 'why' and 'how' questions and look for solutions. All four British early years curricula promote the use of creative and critical thinking skills to solve problems and practitioners are expected to foster independence by asking children to come up with and facilitate their own ideas. This means helping children to develop intrinsic motivation by encouraging them to get involved, have a go and keep trying.

Problem solving involves the following skills and concepts:

- Being able to identify what the problem is

- Understanding that changing something may make a difference

- Being able to generate ideas

- Being open to new ideas and able to take on the ideas of others

- Being able to find links between different pieces of information and connect ideas

- Being able to plan, make decisions and select appropriate resources to accomplish a task

- Being able to verbally express ideas and explain reasoning

- Being willing to have a go and persist at trying again.

Present children with problems and guide them by asking questions such as, 'how can we find out? and 'what do we need to do?' to help them come up with creative solutions.

Activity 1: Litter bugs

Type of activity: Adult-led, whole group followed up with small groups.

Resources: Digital camera, photos showing the effect of litter on wildlife and the environment (litter lying around outdoors and in rivers and wildlife harmed by litter), children's gardening gloves, litter pickers, outdoor bins, resources to make posters and signs.

What to do: Take photos of rubbish lying around the vicinity of your setting and use these to provoke a discussion with the children about littering. Ask the children why littering is bad and encourage them to explain how it affects people, animals and the environment. Support the discussion with photos. Do the children have any ideas how the problem of littering around the setting can be solved? Help the children put their ideas into action by providing the resources and equipment they need.

Key vocabulary: Litter, rubbish, dirty, harm, kill, animals, rivers, fish, wildlife, danger, bin, dispose, clean up, pollution, sight, landscape.

Extension ideas: Raise the issue of the effect that landfill sites and rubbish incinerators have on the environment and talk about recycling. Help the children set up a recycling system in the setting. Introduce them to composting.

HOME LINKS

Ask parents to encourage their children to develop independence by giving them small responsibilities at home such as sweeping up the leaves in the yard, watering garden plants, feeding pets and sorting the recycling.

Activity 2: Block it out

Type of activity: Adult-initiated, during independent play.

Resources: Objects and materials that can be used to build a den or section off an area.

What to do: Bring the children together and explain that it would be lovely if they could help create a quiet area outside where they can sit and rest, talk, read and play quietly. Ask the children for ideas about where the quiet area should be and why. Ask them to suggest how it should be marked out and if it should be cordoned off and with what. Do the children have any ideas for what they can use to block or muffle sound?

Help the children experiment with setting up tents, building dens and creating barriers. Assist them as they try out different materials to block out sound.

Key vocabulary: Noise, sound, quiet, space, block, muffle, barrier, den, shield.

Extension ideas: Challenge the children to create a dark area by blocking out light.

Activity 3: Wasting water

Type of activity: Adult-led, whole group, later divided into small groups.

Resources: Large containers, water butts, watering cans, hosepipes, guttering.

What to do: Do this activity in the summer months. Bring the children together and explain that you have been told there is a water shortage and you are no longer allowed to water the plants with water from the tap. Ask the children if they know where water comes from and how you might be able to collect some. Work through their suggestions and discuss why some are more workable than others. Encourage the children to think about how they can set up equipment outside to collect rainwater. Help the children put their ideas into action.

Key vocabulary: Water, shortage, drought, rain, collect, container, barrel, pipes, gutters, taps, water butt, watering can, hose pipe.

Extension ideas: Ask the children to think about how they can save water in other ways.

Challenge the children to think of ways to save water.

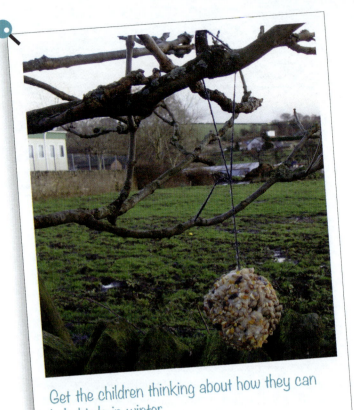

Get the children thinking about how they can help birds in winter.

Activity 5: Long winter

Type of activity: Adult-led, small groups.

Resources: Lard, crisped rice, bird seed, string, pine cones, bird feeders, bird table or resources to make a bird table.

What to do: Bring the children together to discuss why it is more difficult for birds to survive in the winter months. Help the children identify the problems birds come up against, for example, hard ground, lack of insects and soft fruits, and frozen water. Ask the children for ideas about what they can do to help the birds at this time.

Ask the children to suggest how they can find out more about what birds need. Point them toward information books and the internet. The RSPB provides comprehensive guidance (www.rspb.org.uk/ makeahomeforwildlife/advice/helpingbirds/).

Follow the children's direction and help them set up a safe feeding area for birds. Show them how to make bird feeders by crushing crisped rice into lard, squashing it onto pinecones and rolling it in seed.

Key vocabulary: Birds, winter, cold, frozen, food, live, die, healthy, hungry, feed, help, drink, water, seed, insects, grubs.

Extension ideas: Ask the children for ideas about how they can stop other animals eating the bird food. Do they have any ideas about how they can keep the food dry?

Activity 4: Somewhere dry

Type of activity: Adult-led, during independent play.

Resources: Cuddly toy (preferably an animal from the British countryside such as a squirrel, badger or owl), objects and materials that can be used to build a den.

What to do: Place a toy animal outside and make it look as though it is trying to shelter underneath something. Leave it out in the rain over a weekend. When the children to discover it on their return to the setting make a fuss over the animal and ask the children how it must be feeling. Encourage them to explain what is wrong and suggest what they can do to help.

Help the children to develop their ideas and carry out their plans. If the children suggest bringing the animal in, ask them why, where they plan to put it and how they plan to take care of it. Ask the children if wild animals would prefer to live indoors or outside and why. If the children suggest building it a dry shelter outside, help by providing the resources and materials they ask for. Get them to consider the materials' various properties in relation to intended use.

Key vocabulary: Rain, wet, shelter, cold, dry, material, waterproof, warm, strong, outside, indoors, home, house, safe.

Extension ideas: Help the children find out more about the animal and follow their direction as they take the project further.

Encourage children to come up with solutions to problems.

Enhancing continuous provision

Present problems and set up challenges around the outdoor area. Use playground chalk to write on the floor, erect easels or leave whiteboards introducing and explaining challenges and problems.

As the children set about tackling the challenges see if they are able to explain what the problem is. Find out if they have any

ideas about what they need to do to solve it. Help the children to formulate questions that will focus their investigations and connect different ideas. Encourage them to work together and assist them by joining in their conversations and offering comments and questions that challenge their ideas and preconceptions. Listen to them as they work and help by providing the resources and materials they need to facilitate their ideas. Provide information books and help the children research on the internet to find more ideas.

Area of provision	Enhancements that foster problem solving skills
Water	Fill a large container with water and place an empty container a few metres away. Provide a range of holey objects including sieves, colanders, slotted spoons and dish drainers. Challenge the children to, Move the water from one container to the other. Freeze a character from Disney's *Frozen* in a large chunk of ice. Challenge the children to free it.
Sand	Create a seaside habitat: Set a large bowl into damp sand and fill it with water. Add some seaweed, shells and pebbles. Place some toy fish in the 'rock pool' and put some toy crabs on the sand. Challenge the children to, Keep the fish safe from the crabs or Stop the sand falling into the pool.
Construction	Challenge the children to, Build a tower that cannot be knocked down, Build a bridge using found objects or Build a dome shaped building (such as an igloo) using rectangular blocks.
Role Play	On holiday: Place three suitcases and three toy characters next to a large a heap of clothing. Pose the problem, We are going on holiday but do not know what to pack. In each suitcase stick cards that ask the children to, Pack for a skiing holiday, Pack for a beach holiday and Pack for a walking holiday.
Investigation	Put a cuddly toy somewhere out of reach and hang a sign around it's neck saying 'Help!' Leave a full suitcase with a label attached saying 'Lost Property' for the children to discover.
Physical	Pose physical challenges that involve children taking on manageable tasks with each other's help. For example, Find a way to climb up a slide, Find a way to fit as many children as possible in a large cardboard box or Get from one end of a space to the other without touching the floor.
Garden	Challenge the children to paint a picture using nothing but natural objects and materials. What will they use for a brush? How will they make coloured paint? Challenge the children to think of ways to attract wildlife such as bees, birds and hedgehogs into the setting garden.

Curriculum links

Problem solving covers the following areas of learning and development:

EYFS	Talks about why things happen and how things work (UW). Is confident to try new activities, speak in a familiar group, and will talk about their ideas and choose the resources they need; maintains attention and concentrates; works as part of a group and negotiates without aggression (PSED). Uses talk to organise and clarify thinking and ideas; listens and responds to ideas expressed by others (CL).
NIC	Asks questions and talks about why things happen (WAU). Shows a positive attitude towards learning; shows some self-control and expresses feelings and emotions appropriately (PDMU). Talks about their work and things they have made; shares thoughts and ideas with different audiences (LL).
SCE	Values the opportunity to be part of a group in a variety of situations; helps to encourage learning and confidence in others (HW). Uses curiosity and imagination to solve design problems (AD). Shares experiences, ideas and information in a way that communicates their message (LE).
WFPF	Thinks creatively and imaginatively (KUW). Shows curiosity and develops positive attitudes to new experiences and learning; becomes an independent thinker and learner; forms relationships and feels confident to play and work cooperatively (PSD). Talks/communicates, spontaneously and through structured activities, for a variety of purposes, expressing thoughts and ideas (LLC). Uses a variety of materials and tools for experimentation and problem solving (CD).

Recording

There are many different forms of scientific recording. The most obvious that spring to mind are those methods used for recording the results of scientific experiments such as charts, tables and graphs. However, scientific recording is also about documenting observations, thoughts and ideas.

In the foundation stage children should be asked to record their observations and thoughts using pictures, poems and stories. However, it is also important to introduce the use of tables, graphs and charts for sorting and classifying statistical data, as well as recording the results of experiments and investigations.

Recording involves the following skills and concepts:

- Being able to identify and describe the features of places, objects, materials and living things

- Being able to record thoughts and ideas through the use of pictures, poems and stories

- Understanding that information can be recorded using tables, graphs, charts and diagrams

- Being able to use a table, graph, chart or diagram to record information.

The following activities introduce various recording methods that can be used with very young children. These include pictorial and written forms, as well as simple tally charts and pictograms. The outdoor environment provides a rich source of scientific phenomena for children to observe, explore and record their thoughts and ideas about. It is also a great setting for enjoyable, hands-on investigations that provide a meaningful context for practising more formal methods of recording.

Activity 1: The best filter

Type of activity: Adult-led, small groups.

Resources: Water, soil, clear plastic jug, spoon, clear plastic beaker, filter paper, cheap plastic sieves, fabric, paper towel, large piece of card, marker pen, scissors, digital camera, printer, glue, sellotape.

What to do: Mix a small amount of soil into a jug of clean water.

Show this to the children and explain you are going to carry out an experiment to find out which material works best to filter and clean the water.

Begin by passing the different materials around so the children can examine them and predict which will work the best.

Then choose a child to hold a sieve over an empty beaker whilst another pours the muddy water through the sieve into the beaker. Take a photo as they do this, then take another of the filtered water in the beaker. Discuss the results with the children and ask them if they can explain why the water is still very dirty.

Repeat with the filter paper, fabric and paper towel.

Print off the photos. Bring the children together to create a table of results.

Draw a table outline on a large piece of card. Divide the first column into four and invite the children to cut out a piece of filter paper, fabric, paper towel and plastic sieve to stick in each section. Alongside these, stick the photos of the water being poured through each material as well as the photos of the filtered water. Ask the children to read the results from the table and identify which were the best and worst materials to filter the dirty water.

Key vocabulary: Water, soil, dirty, clean, filter, holes, big, small, through, beaker, pour, table, record, results, best, worst.

Extension ideas: Invite the children to choose and test different filtering materials.

Help children make their own nature storybooks.

Activity 2: The story of...

Type of activity: Adult-led, small groups.

Resources: A *Nature Storybook* (Walker Books), digital camera, printer, laminator, scissors, glue, clipboard, paper and pen.

What to do: Read a nature storybook to the children. Take the children outside and explain you would like them to help write their own nature story. Help them to choose a focus. It could be about the weather, current season, a minibeast or natural objects such as soil, grass or trees. Focus in on the subject, observe and explore it closely. Help the children take photos. Ask them to describe what they see, hear, smell and feel and use questions to prompt them to tell you what they know about the subject. Note down what they say.

Print off the photos and stick each picture onto a piece of A4 paper, leaving space underneath to write a sentence or two. Bring the children together to look at the photos and write a simple nature story. Refer to the notes you took outside to remind them what they said and use information books to find out more about the subject. Laminate and bind the finished books.

Key vocabulary: Nature, observe, look, see, sound, feel, smell, what? why? how? where? describe, explain, story, facts, information.

Extension ideas: Share each of the storybooks with the rest of the group. Place them on a rug outside for the children to flick through.

HOME LINKS

Ask parents to take the whole family to a playground and take photos of the different family members having a go at using the whole range of available equipment. Explain they should later share the photos with their children and discuss each family member's age, size and physical ability in relation to the types of equipment they were able to play on.

Go outside and describe what you can see, hear, smell, feel and taste.

Activity 3: Draw it

Type of activity: Adult-initiated, during independent play.

Resources: Clipboards, paper, pencils, coloured pencils, bug viewers, magnifiers.

What to do: Draw the children's attention to details and features of objects, plants and living things outside. Encourage them to talk about and describe what they can see. Start up conversations about interesting architecture, unusual minibeasts or the colours and shapes of plants and flowers.

Provide drawing materials and encourage the children to do observational drawings of the things that interest them. Ask them to talk about and explain their drawings. Help them to add labels.

Key vocabulary: Observe, see, look closely, colour, shape, what is it? Explain, describe, detail, label.

Extension ideas: Provide child-friendly digital cameras for the children to take their own observational photos of what interests them.

Activity 4: Out and about

Type of activity: Adult-led, small groups.

Resources: *Olly and Me Out and About* by Shirley Hughes, clipboard, paper and pen, digital camera.

What to do: Choose a selection of poems from Shirley Hughes' *Olly and Me Out and About* that reflect the current weather and scenery outside. Read these with the children and take time to look at and discuss the pictures. Explain you are going to help the children record their thoughts about being outside in a poem of their own.

Go outside and play for a while. Run around in the wind, splash in puddles, catch snowflakes in your mouth, kick leaves or dance in the sunshine. Ask the children to describe what they can see, hear, feel, smell and taste. Use a clipboard to write down their words and descriptions. Take some photographs and video the children's movements.

Go back inside and talk about what you have just been doing. Read back some of what the children said outside. Show them the photographs and video. Use this to help the children compose a poem about the weather that day.

Key vocabulary: Weather, describe, feel, smell, sound, hear, see, sight, taste, words, poem, record.

Extension ideas: Laminate and bind the poems to make a weather poetry book.

Activity 5: Snap shot

Type of activity: Adult-led, whole group or small groups depending on locality of frogspawn and how easy it is to visit on a regular basis.

Resources: Transport and adult supervision for a trip off-site, child-friendly digital cameras, fishing nets, specimen containers.

What to do: In early March search for a place nearby where there is likely to be some frogspawn. The National Trust shares some ideas about where to find frog spawn (www.nationaltrust.org.uk/article-1355824255053/).

Take the children on a visit to find the frogspawn, scoop some up and examine it closely.

Return to the site regularly to watch the frogspawn develop into tadpoles and eventually frogs. Help the children to document the changes by taking photos at each visit.

Key vocabulary: Frogspawn, jelly, egg, tadpole, legs, tail, swim, frog, change, lifecycle.

Extension ideas: Create a display about the lifecycle of a frog using the photos taken during the visits.

Enhancing continuous provision

Encourage children to independently record the scientific phenomena they see and experience when outside. Provide dictaphones so they can record their own thoughts and child-friendly cameras so they can photograph the things they see. Give them clipboards with paper and coloured pencils so they can draw pictures and write notes. Provide examples of charts, diagrams, graphs and tables for them to look at.

Area of provision	Enhancements that demonstrate recording methods and encourage children to record
Water	Display diagrams of ships and submarines with labels identifying their different parts. Provide laminated chart templates and whiteboard markers so children can experiment with recording results from their own experiments with water such as floating and sinking or filling and emptying.
Sand	Bury sorting objects in the sand and lay out out labelled hoops for the children to sort and classify them.
Construction	Display laminated architectural drawings. Provide clipboards, paper and pens for children to draw and label their own designs. Use playground chalk to draw out a pictogram of favourite construction materials. Invite children to place a piece from their favourite kit in the relevant column.
Role Play	Nature detectives: Provide magnifiers, bug viewers, nets, buckets and baskets for children to explore the outdoor area and collect specimens. Provide photocopied templates of tables and charts with clipboards and pencils for the children to record what they see.
Investigation	Create a three dimensional chart using blocks and leave it for the children to look at, copy, dismantle and rearrange. For example, stick photos of the children's faces on the blocks. Place laminated pictures of 'colour splashes' on the floor to represent hair colour. Stack the children's picture blocks in front of each colour. The towers will show how many children have each hair colour.
Physical	Hang large blackboards and provide coloured chalk for children to draw and write. Provide crayons and paper for children to do rubbings.
Garden	Make a pictorial growth chart. Plant beans or sunflowers and take photos of them every few days. Stick the photos in sequence on the inside of a window facing out. Label the photos with the number of days underneath. Hang a large blackboard and use waterproof chalk pens to create changeable word walls that reflect current interests and topics. Set up a snail race and erect a whiteboard chart nearby where the children can record the results.

Curriculum links

Recording covers the following areas of learning and development:

EYFS	Builds up a vocabulary that reflects the breadth of their experiences; uses talk to organise, sequence and clarify thinking and ideas (CL). Attempts to write short sentences in meaningful contexts (L). Creates simple representations of events, people and objects (EAD).
NIC	Recalls and describes; talks about ideas represented in drawings; uses ICT to present and communicate ideas; writes in a range of genres with teacher guidance (LL). Uses direct experiences, memory and imagination to observe and respond to the world; begins to use visual language to describe what has been examined and observed (AD).
SCE	Develops the skills of scientific inquiry and investigation using practical techniques (S). Inspired by a range of stimuli, and working on own and/or with others, can express and communicate ideas, thoughts and feelings through art, design role play and musical activities (EA). Enjoys exploring interesting materials for writing and different ways of recording experiences and feelings, ideas and information (LE). Enjoys taking photographs or recording sound to represent experiences and the world (T).
WFPF	Makes observations and measurements and keeps records; sorts and groups information using ICT on some occasions (KUW). Collects data for a variety of defined purposes and from a variety of sources, including ICT; represents collected data initially using real objects, pictures or diagrams, progressing to a variety of simple charts, graphs, diagrams, tables or databases (M).

Interpreting

Interpreting is all about making sense of scientific enquiry. It is about looking at the information gathered during an investigation, analysing it and deciding what it means. Being able to interpret scientific findings is important because it allows the investigator to use the information gained. Children learn how to interpret scientific findings by talking about what they see and experience. Early years practitioners play a vital role in this by scaffolding conversation with questioning that develops discussion and sustains shared thinking.

Interpreting involves the following skills:

- Being able to find links between different pieces of information and connect ideas

- Being able to draw upon knowledge and experience to offer an explanation

- Being able to verbally express ideas and explain reasoning

- Being open to new ideas and able to take on the ideas of others.

Just as in the case of hypothesising and predicting this aspect of science is closely related to communication and language, and practitioners can support children by helping them develop the language skills they need to be able to verbalise thinking and explain reasoning. This means allowing plenty of time to talk during scientific exploration. The outdoor environment is the ideal setting for busy conversation and in-depth discussion because young children have a tendency to raise their voices when they disagree with each other. Adults can misinterpret such heated discussion when it occurs in a confined space, however outside children do not necessarily need to keep their voices down, allowing them the freedom to engage in and manage their own noisy debate.

Activity 1: Whys and wherefores

Type of activity: Adult-initiated, during independent play.

Resources: Magnifiers, bug viewers.

What to do: Take the children on a minibeast hunt. Focus their attention on where they find each particular creature. Help the children think about the environment the minibeasts are living in and what this might say about them. For example, why are woodlice found under pieces of rotting wood?

Help the children develop their thinking further by prompting them to describe the habitats and talk about why the minibeasts might like them. For example, why do snails like smooth hard surfaces? Get the children thinking about the location of each minibeast in relation to its physical design. For example, why are flies found on walls and worms found in the ground?

Key vocabulary: Minibeast, live, habitat, environment, body, legs, climb, slither, smooth, crawl, damp, dark, wet, fly, move, where? why? Reason, explain.

Use the information: Help the children create attractive areas for minibeasts to move in based on the information they have learned.

Find out about minibeasts and use the information to make them suitable homes.

Activity 2: Christmas ice decorations

Type of activity: Adult-led, small groups.

Resources: Christmas silicone moulds, glitter, metallic craft shapes, sparkly string, food colouring, jugs of water, pipettes, freezer, towels, Christmas trees for indoors and outdoors.

What to do: Explain you would like the children to make some ice decorations for the Christmas tree. Provide silicone moulds and pipettes for them to fill with water and drops of food colouring. Provide glitter and sparkly objects for them to add. Cut pieces of sparkly string and place one end of each piece in a mould, leaving the other end to hang over the side. Take the children with you to watch as you place the moulds in a freezer. Leave them overnight.

The following day take the children with you to take the moulds out of the freezer. Ask them to explain what has happened to the water. Do they know why?

Set up a small Christmas tree inside, arrange some towels around the base and decorate it with the ice decorations. Then take some and hang them on a tree outside. Draw the children's attention to them throughout the day. Compare the decorations on the trees inside and outdoors. Can the children explain what is happening and why? What have the children learned about water and ice?

Key vocabulary: Water, freeze, frozen, ice, cold, warm, melt, sunshine, freezer, inside, outside.

Use the information: Make more ice decorations and help the children choose the best place to display them based upon what they have learned about freezing and melting.

Activity 3: Let's go fly a kite

Type of activity: Adult-led, small groups.

Resources: A variety of different shaped kites.

What to do: Take the children out to a wide open space on a windy day to fly kites. Try different designs such as box kites, novelty kites, traditional diamond shaped kites and delta kites.

Encourage the children to watch and compare how the different kites fly. Can the children explain what is keeping each kite in the air? Why do they think some stay up longer than others? Do the different designs make the kites fly in different ways?

Key vocabulary: Kite, fly, air, wind, float, breeze, dive, zoom, fast, slow, hover, crash, design, shape.

Use the information: Help the children to use the information they have learned to create some simple designs and make their own kites.

Test different paints to find out which makes the best hand prints.

Activity 5: Messing with paint

Type of activity: Adult-initiated, during independent play.

Resources: Large roll of white paper, large stones to hold it down, poster paint, powder paint, finger paints, watercolours, large shallow containers, paintbrushes, aprons, leaves.

What to do: Lay out a large sheet of white paper and challenge the children to make a big handprint collage. Provide different types of paint for the children to use and experiment with.

As they dip their hands in the paint ask them to describe how it feels. As they make prints on the paper, encourage them to evaluate how well the print has come out. Are the children able to explain why some prints are coming out better than others?

Allow the children to mix their own paints and create different consistencies by adding more or less water.

Key vocabulary: Thick, thin, runny, wet, watery, powder, add, less, more, print, paint, dark, faint, patchy.

Use the information: Start again and create another collage but this time print with leaves. This time ask the children to help choose and mix the paints using the information they have learned about which type of paint and consistency works best.

Activity 4: Rainbow celery

Type of activity: Adult-led, small groups.

Resources: Large tall clear plastic tumblers, leafy celery (preferably with roots attached), food colouring, pipettes, scissors.

What to do: Show the children some celery and ask if they know what it is. Explain how celery grows in the ground and point out the roots. Trim the bottom off a stick and show the children the holes at the bottom. Pass it around for them to have a closer look.

Half fill some clear plastic tumblers with water. Give the children some pipettes and ask them to add plenty of food colouring to each tumbler. Snip the bottom off more celery stalks and invite the children to place one stalk in each tumbler. Ask the children what they think might happen.

Leave the celery in clear view and revisit it regularly throughout the day. As the stalks begin to draw up the coloured water, ask the children if they can explain what is happening. Encourage discussion and debate but do not give them an explanation yet.

Bring the stalks inside overnight and revisit them the following morning when the colouring has traveled further up. Do the children have any more ideas about what is happening?

Go outside and look closely at some flowers and plants. Pull up a couple of plants to look at the roots. Do the children know what plant roots are for? Are they able to explain how plants drink water?

Key vocabulary: Plant, grow, water, drink, suck, draw, up, colour, explain, reason, why?

Use the information: Set up growing experiments to demonstrate how important water is for growth and survival. Plant seeds and water some but not others to see which germinate and which do not. Set out some young tomato plants and water some but not others so the children can see plants wilt and die when they do not get what they need.

Don't forget to think about…

…giving children time to talk. Plan for quality over quantity, or in other words, try not to squeeze too much into each day. Plan less activities in order to allow sufficient time for in-depth discussion and make space in the timetable for children to reflect upon what they have learned through self-directed play.

Enhancing continuous provision

Encourage children to interpret the information they gain whilst playing and exploring outside by asking them to describe what they can see and explain what is going on. Get the children making connections and explaining their reasoning by using questions such as 'can you tell me what is happening?', 'why do you think that is happening?', 'how do you know that?', 'what do you think that means?' and 'do you agree?'

Area of provision	Enhancements that encourage children to interpret
Water	Cut the tops off some plastic bottles and fill them half way with coloured water. Put them in different places around the outdoor area. Draw the children's attention to the bottles on a regular basis and prompt discussion about why some are more full than others. Helpful questions/comments include: Can you explain where the water has gone? Look, there is more water there than yesterday! Where do you think the water came from?
Sand	Provide three trays filled with dry sand, damp sand and sopping wet sand with a range of sand toys. Helpful questions/comments include: Why is it so difficult to build a sandcastle with dry/sopping wet sand? You really are having to squash that damp sand through the sieve.
Construction	Draw attention to the design of physical space and help children make links between how something is made, its purpose and intended use. Helpful questions/comments include: Why do we need stairs here? How do we use our hands to open the gate? What would happen if that bench only had three legs? What a useful railing.
Role Play	Science laboratory: Set up a table and provide white lab coats, goggles, plastic beakers, funnels, flasks, petri dishes and pipettes along with a variety of substances and liquids such as flour, powder paint, couscous, cornflakes, baking powder, water, oil, vinegar, washing up liquid and carbonated water. Helpful questions/comments include: Why does… happen when you mix… with…? What do you think made that happen? Look how soggy that is now.
Investigation	Set up a pot and pan drum kit. Use saucepans, frying pans, plastic tupperware, big thick ceramic plant pots and wooden, plastic and metal spoons. Helpful questions/comments include: What type of beater do you need to make a deep/high sound? Why do metal pans make a different sound to ceramic pots? That is a very loud/quiet sound.
Physical	Provide a selection of ride-on vehicles (with and without pedals), tricycles, scooters and sit-on rockers. Helpful questions/comments include: What do you need to do to make it go forwards/backwards? How do you make it slow down/speed up? How does it work? What happens if you push harder? Wow, you are making that move really fast!
Garden	Provide a foot pump and large selection of balloons. Allow the children to experiment with using the pump to blow up the balloons and see what happens. Helpful questions/comments include: Why did the balloon burst? Why did the balloon shoot off the end of the nozzle? Look what is happening to the balloon.

Curriculum links

Interpreting covers the following areas of learning and development:

EYFS	Talks about why things happen and how things work; makes observations of objects, materials and living things and explains why some things occur, and talks about changes (UW). Uses talk to connect ideas and explain what is happening; listens and responds to ideas expressed by others (CL).
NIC	Asks questions and talks about why things happen (WAU). Asks questions, describes and explains; answers questions to give information and demonstrate understanding; offers reasons to support opinions given; shares thoughts and ideas with different audiences (LL).
SCE	Develops the skills of scientific inquiry and investigation using practical techniques (S). Values the opportunity to be part of a group in a variety of situations (HW). Asks questions and links learning with what they already know; shares experiences and feelings, ideas and information in a way that communicates their messages (LE).
WFPF	Sees links between cause and effect; recognises simple patterns in their findings; describes what they have found out and offers simple explanations (KUW). Talks/communicates, spontaneously and through structured activities, for a variety of purposes, expressing thoughts and ideas (LLC).

Reflecting and evaluating

Reflection is the easier of these two higher order skills and involves encouraging children to look back at what they did and what they learned. Age-appropriate ways of doing this with foundation stage children include the use of stories and displays. Evaluation is a much more difficult skill because it requires children to think back and decide if they would have done anything differently. Young children find this easier when reflecting upon artwork because they have a visual end result that they can evaluate in terms of appearance and think about how they could make it better. In science, however, evaluation is more abstract because children are expected to think about what they did, how it impacted upon the outcome and what they need to do next time to improve it.

Reflecting and evaluating involve the following skills and concepts:

- Being able to think back and recall an experience

- Being able to retell experiences in sequence and in detail

- Being able to interpret scientific findings (explain why something might have happened)

- Understanding cause and effect (that changing something may have an affect on something else)

- Being able to think of new ideas that will solve problems and improve outcomes.

Observation records are an extremely powerful tool for helping young children to reflect and evaluate. Visual cues such as photos and video can be used to help children revisit and re-experience their scientific investigations. Just like a piece of artwork this gives children something concrete to look at, a visual record that they can use to help them evaluate their learning.

Method 1: Learning story

Purpose: To revisit the activity with the children and help them reflect upon what they learned.

Resources: Digital camera, observation notes, computer, printer, laminator, comb binder.

What to do: During a scientific investigation take photos of the children, listen to their conversations and note down their thoughts, questions and ideas. Use these photos and observation notes to make a learning story.

Create a comic strip with photos accompanied by a narrative explaining what the children did during their investigation. Then insert speech bubbles containing the children's comments and questions. Print, laminate and bind into a book.

Read the story to the whole group. Pause now then to ask the children if they can remember what they were thinking during the investigation.

Can they explain what they were doing? Do they know the answers to any of their questions now? What have they learned?

Key questions: Can you explain…? How did you…? What were you thinking? What did you find out? What did you learn?

Use learning displays to nudge children's memories and prompt discussion.

Method 2: Learning display

Purpose: To help children revise and consolidate learning and evaluate the outcomes of an activity.

Resources: Low level display board, digital camera, observation notes, computer, printer, staple gun, sellotape or drawing pins.

What to do: This works in the same way as a learning story but is presented as a display. Photos and observations are mounted on a display board at child-eye level and practitioners bring children to the display to look at it and discuss the featured activity. There is opportunity here to bring small groups of children to the display together and open up discussion about what happened and what they might do next time.

Key questions: Can you remember? Can you explain…? What were you doing? What happened? Why do you think that happened? What went wrong? What might you do differently next time?

Take it outside: Create this display on an outdoor display board or on the inside of a window facing out.

Method 3: Group discussion

Purpose: To encourage children to talk about what they did, evaluate the outcome and think about what they would do differently next time.

Resources: Items or photos from the investigation or activity.

What to do: As soon as possible after a scientific investigation bring the children together to discuss what happened.

Invite volunteers to explain what they did during the activity. Use items and observation photos to nudge the children's memories and help them recount the details. Ask if they can explain why they were doing the activity, what happened and why.

Key questions: Can you explain what you did? What were you trying to do/find out? What did you use? Why did you use that? Could you have used anything else? Did anything go wrong? Did anything surprise you?

Don't forget to think about…

…helping children understand the value of making mistakes. Getting something wrong should be seen as a valuable learning experience. Children who are able to identify mistakes and think of alternative ways of doing things are very creative thinkers.

Photo books are a great way of helping children to reflect.

Method 4: Photo book

Purpose: To revisit the activity with the children and help them reflect upon what they learned.

Resources: Digital camera, computer, printer, laminator, comb binder.

What to do: This type of book is useful for helping children reflect upon an off-site visit. During the visit note down the children's comments and questions. Take photos and invite the children to use the camera and take photos too. Use a computer to create a template with space for a photo and text below. Sit with the children, look through the photos and encourage them to think back to the visit. Use your observation notes to prompt discussion and help the children reflect upon what they learned. Type their comments below each photo. Print, laminate and bind into a book.

Share the book with the whole group and use it to encourage the children to talk about what they saw and found out during the trip. Leave the book in the book corner for the children to flick through independently.

Key questions: Can you remember? What did you see? What were you doing? What were you thinking? What did you find out? What did you learn? What was the best bit?

Method 5: Mind-mapping

Purpose: To help children see their learning by showing them what they knew before and what they know now.

Resources: Large pieces of card, marker pens.

What to do: Bring the children together before starting an science investigation to find out what they know about the subject. Ask them questions and record their answers on a mind-map. Use these questions and answers to help shape the investigation. Help the children to decide what they would like to know and what they need to do in order to find out.

At the end of the investigation, bring the children together again to revisit the mind-map and find out what they have learned. Look at the original questions and read back some of their answers. Ask the children if they were correct or not. Encourage them to explain what they found out during the investigation and how this was different to what they know now.

Key questions: What do you know about…? What is…? Have you seen… before? What did you find out about…? What have you learned about…? Were you right about that?

Method 6: Watch it back

Purpose: To give children an opportunity to re-experience the activity, reflect upon what happened and evaluate outcomes.

Resources: Video camera, computer.

What to do: Video record the children as they investigate something then play it back to them so they can watch what happened. It is best to bring the children to the video one at a time or in pairs. Play the recording once, allowing the children to comment at will. Then play the recording a second time but pause every so often to explore interesting comments or questions the children either made at the time of the investigation or while watching it back. Help the children to reflect upon what happened and ask them if there is anything they would change or add to the investigation if they were to do it again.

Key questions: What are you doing there? Why did you do that? What happened next? If you could do it again, what else would you try/what would you change? What might have happened if…?

Tip…

…Time moves on quickly for young children so it is best to reflect upon and evaluate an activity as soon as possible afterwards, while it is still fresh in their minds.

Enhancing continuous provision

Help to make reflection and evaluation part of everyday conversation by displaying questions and comments that practitioners can refer to when starting up reflective discussions with the children. Print off, laminate and display open-ended questions on the inside of windows facing out, set up easels or A Boards next to activities with question ideas and conversation starters, or simply write questions and comments on the floor with playground chalk. Find some suggestions for helpful questions and comments in the table below:

Area of provision	Helpful questions and comments that encourage children to reflect and evaluate
Water	Did that container hold enough water? The water went everywhere. What could you have used instead? Was it easy to stop the water escaping? What would you use next time? What did you need? Shall we try again? Why do you think that happened? That doesn't look very full.
Sand	That looked like hard work. What did you use? Why did you use that? Can you think of anything that would have made it easier? What were you trying to do? Can you think of another way to do that? Why won't the sand do what you want it to do? Look at how the sand is crumbling away.
Construction	I see you used… Why did you use those? Is there anything else you could have used? Is that the best kit for making a vehicle? What kit would you use next time? Was it easier to use… or…? What if you were to try…? Did you have a plan? That looks sturdy.
Role Play	That is a good idea. What made you think of that? What could you use instead? That looked like it worked well. Have you ever been…? Have you ever seen…? How do you know about…? Different people do things in different ways.
Investigation	That looks interesting. Why do you think that happened? What do you think caused that? Why didn't you do it another way? Look what happened. Why didn't you use…? Are you going to have another go? Do you remember what happened last time? Do you have any other ideas?
Physical	You must have good balance. Why don't you think you were able to do that? Is there anything you could have done to make that easier? Look at how… is doing it. Do you think that was safe? Can you think of a safer way to do that? What if you were to use something else?
Garden	What did you plant? Why do you think it hasn't grown? What do you need to do next time? That soil is very dry. Those flowers don't look very happy. How can we make our minibeast hotel more attractive to woodlice? Why isn't that windmill turning in the wind?

Curriculum links

Reflecting and evaluating cover the following areas of learning and development:

EYFS	Understands and answers 'how' and 'why' questions; questions why things happen and gives explanations; talks about past and present events; talks about why things happen and how things work (UW). Uses talk to organise, sequence and clarify thinking, ideas and events (CL).
NIC	Recalls, describes, explains; retells events or personal experiences in sequence with reasonable detail; listens and responds to adults and peers; answers questions to give information and demonstrate understanding; offers reasons to support opinions given (LL).
SCE	Develops the skills of scientific inquiry and investigation using practical techniques (S). Listens or watches for useful or interesting information and uses this to make choices or learn new things; asks questions and links learning with what they already know (LE).
WFPF	Sees links between cause and effect; recognises simple patterns in their findings; describes what they have found out and offers simple explanations; reflects on and evaluates their own and others' work (KUW). Talks/communicates, spontaneously and through structured activities, for a variety of purposes, expressing thoughts and ideas (LLC).

Presenting

The conclusion of a science project involves communicating findings to others. This final skill of scientific enquiry is very important, both for the children, who consolidate their learning through sharing it with others, and for practitioners, who gain valuable insight into the children's level of understanding about a subject.

Presenting involves the following skills:

- Being able to gather and record information with the use of notes, pictures, photos and digital recordings

- Being able to organise and present visual information in a way that makes it easily accessible to others

- Being able to verbally share information in a way that is clearly understandable to others

- Having the confidence to speak in front of adults and peers.

Again, like in so many other aspects of science, at this stage it is all about developing communication and language skills. Children need to be able to collect and record information during an activity and then collate it and present it to others. As children get older they will be expected to present their findings both verbally and in written form with the use of tables and graphs. In preparation for this, young children need plenty of speaking and listening practice that involves recalling and retelling their experiences and explaining their findings. They should also practise relaying information visually through drawings, paintings and photos, as well as through the use of simple charts and pictograms. The following presentation methods aim to help young children practise these skills. A final method is suggested for practitioners to communicate children's learning to parents.

Method 1: Information book

Purpose: To enable children to share their knowledge and understanding of a subject with others.

Resources: Child-friendly digital cameras, computer, printer, laminator, comb binder, information books.

What to do: Work with the children to create an information book. This can either be an information book or an instructional book.

Information book: Take the children outside and ask if there is anything they would like to find out more about. This could be something natural, a man-made object or a living creature. Help the child to take photos of the thing that interests them. Use a computer to create a template with space for a photo and text below.

Use information books to help the children research their subject and type a simple sentence below each picture.

Instructional book: Choose a subject matter that the children know plenty about, for example, caring for a pet that lives in the setting. Help the children take photos of the subject. Create a template with space for a photo and text below. Ask the children to think of an instruction to go with each photo.

Print out the pages, laminate them and bind them into a book for the children to read and share with others.

Key vocabulary: Photo, camera, book, information, find out, learn, research, tell others, instruct, guide, help, explain how.

Create a digital presentation.

Method 2: Digital presentation

Purpose: To enable children to present their learning to adults and peers.

Resources: Digital camera, computer, projector, presentation software (PowerPoint, Keynote or a child-friendly version such as Present on Tizzy's First Tools).

What to do: Take photos of the children as they investigate something. Note down their comments, questions and thoughts. At the end of the activity upload the photos and set up a template for a digital presentation. Create a set of slides, paste the photos and add speech and thought bubbles containing the comments from your observation notes. Bring the children over. Show them one slide at a time and ask them to explain what is happening in the picture. Read out the text in the speech/thought bubbles to prompt their thinking. Type what the children say onto the slide to create a commentary. When the presentation is complete show it to the whole group. Set the presentation to run during parents' evening or on an open day.

Key vocabulary: Present, presentation, what happened? explain, how?, next, photos, pictures, tell, type, project, show, learn.

Method 3: Show and tell

Purpose: To encourage children to present to each other.

Resources: Object or artefact related to the science investigation or activity.

What to do: This is the most straightforward method of presenting. Bring children to stand at the front, either as individuals or in small groups. Ask them to explain what they did, how they did it and what happened with the help of visual props. For example, they might show the audience some oil, water and marbling inks and explain how they made marbling pictures in puddles. When they are finished invite children in the audience to ask questions.

Key vocabulary: Tell, explain, show, talk about, how?, what?, where?, example, listen, ask, question, answer.

HOME LINKS

Send home the books that you make for the children to read with their parents. Invite parents into the setting to look at displays and presentations. Plan an assembly that involves children presenting to parents.

Create a large-scale floor display.

Method 4: Large-scale art

Purpose: To enable children to present their learning in a creative way.

Resources: Large floor space, playground chalks, water, paintbrushes, natural objects, digital camera.

What to do: Challenge the children to create a large-scale outdoor display. For example, a topic about space may lead to a large picture of the solar system. Black tarmac would be the best background for this. Help the children draw out the outline of the sun, planets and moons using playground chalks. Either use natural resources to collage the sun and planets or crush up some chalk, add water and provide paint brushes for the children to colour them in. Invite the children to look for natural objects that will help complete the picture, for example, stones and rocks for the asteroid belt and white or yellow flowers for stars. Help the children label the picture in chalk. Ask the children if they know any facts about space and record these as short statements inside rocket outlines. Take a photo of the display to keep as a permanent record.

Key vocabulary: Large-scale, picture, display, show, draw, paint, label, create, use, represent, fact, record.

Method 5: Informative display

Purpose: To enable children to present their learning to adults and peers.

Resources: Child-friendly digital camera, observation notes, children's drawings, computer, printer, staple gun or drawing pins.

What to do: Help the children create a display about a scientific investigation. Give them a digital camera to take their own photos during the activity. Ask them to draw pictures and diagrams to show what they did.

Bring them to a computer to tell you what they did, how they did it and what happened. Type their explanations up and print them out.

Mount the photos, pictures and typed comments on a display board. Invite the children to write short labels to add to photos, pictures and diagrams. Use observation records to add captions, speech and thought bubbles to the display.

Key vocabulary: Display, show, what happened? explain, how, next, photos, pictures, diagram, tell, caption, label, type, learn, example.

Tip...

Create displays so that they are at child-eye level. This will encourage children to visit them and spend time talking about what they did with each other. It also makes it easier for them to show parents what they did.

Method 6: Working wall

Purpose: To present children's learning to parents.

Resources: Display board, digital camera, computer, printer, staple gun or drawing pins.

What to do: Create a working display that evolves with a science investigation. Display an initial mind-map of the children's knowledge about the subject. Then as they go about their investigations take photos and add these to the display along with observation notes. Complete the display with an end-of-project mind-map that shows the children's knowledge at the end of the investigation. Invite parents in to see and talk about the display.

Key vocabulary: Display, present, learning, observations, mind-map, learning journey, thoughts, ideas, knowledge, understanding.

Enhancing continuous provision

An important part of presenting is being able to clearly explain things in a way that other people understand. Many young children find this difficult and practitioners can give them plenty of practice on a day-to-day basis by encouraging them to talk about what they are doing and explain their ideas. Display helpful comments and question prompts around the outdoor area that practitioners can refer to when engaging children in these conversations.

In addition, it is a good idea to create spaces for children to set up and organise their own presentations. Ideas include

supplying child-friendly digital cameras for children to take photos and video recordings, creating a stage and providing microphones for children to present to each other, putting up magnetic display boards where children can stick up drawings and diagrams, and providing low level tables where they can display the models they make.

Furthermore, if possible, set up interactive displays on tables outside near the entrance to the setting featuring current topics, projects or investigations that the children can show their parents on the way in and out.

Area of provision	Helpful questions and comments that assist children when they are presenting
Water	What did you use to make your boat? What did you do to make that waterwheel turn? Tell me about what you are doing. How does the ice feel? Do you know how to make slime? Why are you doing it like that?
Sand	Can you describe how the sand feels? What is the best type of sand for building castles? What have you found buried in the sand? Tell me about what you have built. Why don't you take a photo of what you have done?
Construction	Can you explain how you did that? Tell me about the tools you are using. Who did you work with? Who did what? What are you building? How do you know that is going to stay standing? Perhaps you could draw a plan of what you have built.
Role Play	Where did you get that idea from? Tell me about your game. Who are you playing with? What role is… playing? What is the story? What are you using that for? Where is this? Would you like to video your story?
Investigation	How did you make that happen. Can you explain how that works? Tell me about what you can see. What does that do? What have you found out about…? That is an interesting piece of equipment. Can you describe that smell/sound?
Physical	That looks like an interesting game. Are there any rules? What is the aim of the game? What are you trying to do? Why do/don't you think that is a good idea? Can you show me how a… moves? Can you draw a picture of that?
Garden	What have you found there? Can you describe it? What does it look like? Can you describe that pattern/shape? What do you know about…? Why are… so important? Why don't you take some close-up photos of what you have found?

Curriculum links

Presenting covers the following areas of learning and development:

EYFS	Talks about why things happen and how things work (UW). Is confident to speak in a familiar group and will talk about ideas (PSED). Expresses self effectively, showing awareness of listeners' needs; develops own narratives and explanations by connecting ideas or events (CL).
NIC	Expresses themselves with increasing clarity and confidence, using a growing vocabulary and more complex sentence structure; talks about work, play and things they have made; shares thoughts, feelings and ideas with different audiences (LL).
SCE	Develops the skills of scientific inquiry and investigation using practical techniques (S). Has experienced the energy and excitement of presenting for audiences and being part of an audience for other people's presentations (EA). Shares experiences, ideas and information in a way that communicates their message (LE).
WFPF	Communicates observations and measurements; describes what they have found out and offers simple explanations (KUW). Organises and presents factual writing in different ways, using ICT as appropriate; talks/communicates, spontaneously and through structured activities, for a variety of purposes, expressing thoughts and ideas (LLC).

Using technology

Scientists have access to a wide range of technological tools to help them with their investigations and technology has played an important part in scientific discovery. There is no reason why young children cannot use ICT to assist in their own scientific explorations, as well as to record the discoveries they make and present their findings to others.

Using technology involves the following skills and concepts:

- Understanding that technology can be used to advance knowledge and further learning

- Understanding that information can be recorded using technological equipment

- Understanding that information can be collated and presented with the help of computers

- Being able to operate simple ICT equipment

- Being able to navigate simple ICT software programs

- Being able to select a type of technology to assist and serve a particular purpose.

All four British early years curriculum documents set out the expectation that children be given opportunities to interact with and operate ICT equipment and software. Following is a selection of technological tools that can be used to enhance science teaching and learning. This includes ICT equipment that can be used outside, as well as computer software that can be used to collate or present data that has been collected from the outdoor environment.

Resource 1: Digital camera

Science skills: Observing, exploring, gathering information, investigating, following instructions, recording, presenting, reflecting and evaluating.

ICT skills: Operating simple equipment, selecting and using a piece of equipment for a particular purpose, using technology to record and represent experiences.

How it enhances science learning: Children who are provided with child-friendly digital cameras can make observations and gather information without needing the fine motor control and ability to draw and write. Practitioners can also use cameras to photograph children's explorations and use these to re-visit the activity and prompt reflection and discussion later on. Photos are also a valuable assessment record and even more so are video recordings, which not only capture children's self-commentary and conversations word-for-word, but also their vocal intonation and facial expressions.

Key vocabulary: Camera, photo, aim, press, button, on, off, switch, picture, see, show, detail, record, observe, describe.

Give children digital cameras so they can gather information independently.

Resource 2: MP3 recorder

Science skills: Observing, exploring, gathering information, recording and presenting.

ICT skills: Operating simple equipment, selecting and using a piece of equipment for a particular purpose, using technology to record and represent experiences.

How it enhances science learning: Children can use MP3 recording devices to record and play back the interesting sounds they hear whilst outside. This enables them to listen to and analyse unfamiliar sounds over again, as well as play the sounds to others and talk about what they have heard. Children may also use MP3 recorders to record their own thoughts and collect the views of their peers. The recordings children make can be downloaded and used to create digital talking books and presentations.

MP3 recorders are useful teaching tools as well. Practitioners can use them to record sounds for listening games. They can also be used to record conversations with children, which can then be played back and transcribed for assessment purposes.

Key vocabulary: Recorder, dictaphone, press, button, switch, speak, talk, sound, listen, hear, record, play, describe.

Resource 3: Digital microscope

Science skills: Observing, exploring, comparing, measuring, sorting and classifying, gathering information, investigating, recording and presenting.

ICT skills: Exploring and playing with technologies to see what they can do, operating simple equipment, selecting and using a piece of equipment for a particular purpose.

How it enhances science learning: Digital magnifiers enable children to see minute details that the naked eye would otherwise be incapable of perceiving. There are devices on the market, such as the Easi-Scope and Tuff-Scope 2, that are especially designed for young children with simple controls that enable them to take photos and video recordings of magnified images. There are also wireless versions of these available, making it possible to take them outside. Furthermore, they are a useful tool for whole group teaching as practitioners can bring items of interest inside and use a digital microscope to project magnified images onto the interactive whiteboard for close observation and discussion.

Key vocabulary: Magnify, bigger, image, close-up, detail, see, look, photo, record, picture, show, describe, press, button, switch, turn, focus, on, off.

HOME LINKS

Send a cheap digital camera and notebook home with one child each weekend. Give each family an achievable task, such as, Take some photos of interesting minibeasts or Go on a nature walk and take some photos of what you see. On the camera's return print or project the images for everyone to see and ask the child to talk about what they did and saw.

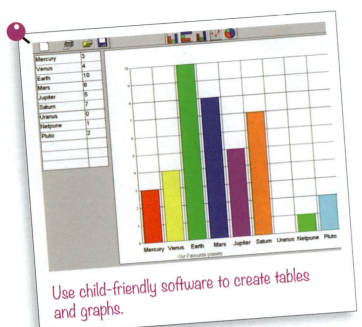

Use child-friendly software to create tables and graphs.

Resource 4: Programmable toys

Science skills: Exploring, questioning, investigating, following instructions, measuring, hypothesising, predicting and problem solving.

ICT skills: Exploring and playing with technologies to see what they can do, operating simple equipment.

How it enhances science learning: Playing with programmable toys is a good way of introducing cause and effect. As they play children will be thinking about where they want the robot to go, how far it needs to travel and what they need to do to make that happen. Perhaps the most accessible programmable toy for young children is the Bee-bot®, which comes with a number of accessories including a trailer, which is a useful aid for teaching about force and movement. There is also scope for learning about friction by asking Bee-bot to travel across different surfaces. Other programmable toys include the Pixie, which is similar to the Bee-bot, even if a little outdated, and the Roamer, which is much bigger and requires more complicated instructions.

Key vocabulary: Program, toy, instruct, press, button, switch, on, off, direction, forward, backward, right, left, turn, over, under, through, around, to, here, there, away, toward, go, stop, up, down, pull, push, move.

Try…

…taking the children on a technology trail. Walk around the local area and spot technological 'big ideas'. Discuss how they make life easier and improve safety and efficiency.

Resource 5: Tablet computer

Science skills: Gathering information, questioning, investigating, measuring, coming up with ideas, recording, interpreting, presenting, reflecting and evaluating.

ICT skills: Gathering information, collecting data, operating simple equipment, selecting and using a piece of equipment for a particular purpose.

How it enhances science learning: There is a wide selection of free or low cost applications available for tablet computers on just about any theme. Download apps and information about current topics, and place tablets in the outdoor reading area for children to look at alongside information books (put up a parasol or tent to shield the sun and make the screens more visible).

Practitioners can also make good use of this technology to take observation notes with accompanying photos and video.

Tablets are also valuable teaching tools, allowing practitioners to play video clips and show children photos during science explorations outside.

Key vocabulary: Tablet, iPad, video, picture, application (app), read, type, find out, switch, button, on, off.

Resource 6: Software

Science skills: Comparing, sorting, classifying, gathering information, questioning, following instructions, coming up with ideas, problem solving, recording, interpreting, presenting, reflecting and evaluating.

ICT skills: Exploring and playing with technologies to see what they can do, collecting data, sorting and grouping information, operating simple software, selecting and using a piece of software for a particular purpose, using technology to record and represent experiences.

How it enhances science learning: There is a wide range of computer software programs that have been designed specifically for young children. Tizzy's First Tools is a versatile resource, providing a platform for creating charts, writing and presenting information. 2Simple is also very useful for science teaching because children can use it to create simple pictograms and graphs. What's more, 2Simple software is currently being developed for use with the iPad, which allows for creating charts and graphs during outdoor activities.

Key vocabulary: Operate, control, navigate, type, press, button, mouse, cursor, information, record, input.

Enhancing continuous provision

It is just as possible to use technological tools indoors as it is outside. There is a wide range of equipment designed for use with very young children, which is robustly built and able to withstand relatively rough handling. Furthermore, most equipment is now wireless and therefore portable, making it possible to use during outdoor science activities. Those pieces of equipment that are either too expensive or too delicate to use outside can still be set up indoors and used to support outdoor learning. For example, children can bring the natural items they collect outside to a digital microscope, which is attached to a computer and projector inside.

Try to provide as many pieces of technological equipment as possible for children to use and enhance their scientific explorations outside. Following are some examples of how this might be done.

Area of provision	Enhancements that demonstrate and make use of technology
Water	Turn the water tray into a pond or rock pool and supply waterproof underwater cameras and torches for children to explore what life is like under water. Display pictures of submarines and the equipment divers use when they go under water.
Sand	Bury small objects made out of various materials and provide metal detectors for the children to search and dig for metal objects. Provide a digital maginifer for children to look at grains of sand up close.
Construction	Challenge the children to build obstacle courses for radio controlled vehicles. Provide construction materials that use technology.
Role Play	Mobile medical clinic: Put up a small gazebo and supply doctor and nurse costumes, medical kits including real stethoscopes, digital thermometers and digital weighing scales. Display x-ray images. Archeological dig: Make some fake building ruins using large wooden blocks and mark out 'interesting' sections with playground chalk. Provide toy cameras, walkie-talkies, mobile phones and tablet computers. Display pictures of ancient ruins and archeologists at work.
Investigation	Use a visualiser to project close-up images of natural objects on the interactive whiteboard. Add handwritten labels to the projected image. Get a small animal eye view: Attach a small video camera to a radio controlled car and send it through tunnels and under hedges to see what it is like.
Physical	Provide digital timers for children to time themselves in races and games. Provide video cameras for children to record each other undertaking challenging physical tasks.
Garden	Collect delicate natural items such as thin and decaying autumn leaves or flower petals and place them on a light box indoors for the children to more clearly see the colours and veins. Provide digital cameras for the children to photograph minibeasts, birds, flowers and plants. Put a webcam inside a bird box and see if anything happens.

Curriculum links

Using technology covers the following areas of learning and development:

EYFS	Knows how to operate simple equipment; knows information can be retrieved from computers; recognises that a range of technology is used in places such as homes and schools; selects and uses technology for particular purposes (UW).
NIC	Is aware of everyday uses of technological tools and know how to use some of these safely (WAU). Uses ICT to present and communicate ideas (LL).
SCE	Enjoys playing with and exploring technologies to discover what they can do and how they can help; explores software and uses what they learn to solve problems and present ideas, thoughts, or information; enjoys exploring and using technologies to communicate with others within and beyond place of learning; enjoys taking photographs or recording sound and images to represent experiences and the world (T).
WFPF	Sorts and groups information using ICT on some occasions (KUW). Experiments with new learning opportunities including ICT (PSD). Collects data for a variety of defined purposes and from a variety of sources, including ICT (MD).

Planning and organising outdoor science

Every setting has a different outdoor environment with particular features and limitations. A large area needs to be designed carefully to ensure the best possible use of space. On the other hand, practitioners with small outdoor areas need to think about how they can make use of nearby public spaces or the possibility of taking regular trips further afield.

When planning and organising outdoor science provision it is important to think about how the outside environment can be utilised to complement and extend the learning that is happening indoors. Outdoor provision is about taking advantage

of the unique characteristics of the outside environment and using them to enhance teaching and learning. Plan physical activities that get children playing with scientific concepts and actively experiencing scientific phenomena.

Plan outdoor learning in the same detail as you would the indoor space. Draw a diagram of both the indoor and outdoor areas including permanent fixtures. Photocopy these and use one for each day of the week. Handwrite planned activities and resources onto the diagrams, ensuring you consider logistics in terms of indoor and outdoor supervision. Take account of where adult-led activities are to be carried out during each session and plan so that adults are occupying both spaces at all times.

If possible, make life easier by setting up early in the morning before the children arrive. Otherwise pass the planning diagram to a support assistant and ask them to set up while the children settle in during the first fifteen minutes of the day.

Science in a large outside space

Practitioners who are lucky enough to have a large space should consider providing the following:

- Resources for physical activities that explore forces and materials, including skittles, balls, ramps, pulleys, climbing frames, swings, slides and ride-on vehicles

- Big construction equipment for children to build on a large scale

- A sheltered area that can be used to learn about science through role-play

- Chalkboards, easels and playground chalks for children to record their thoughts and ideas

- Large sand and water play equipment for children to explore the properties of each on a grand and messy scale

- A soil patch or permanent planters for growing and if possible a greenhouse with perspex windows.

Science in a small outside space

Practitioners who have a smaller space might like to consider providing the following:

- Functional dividers such as large storage containers or planters to make the best possible use of space while sectioning off areas

- Small plant pots and troughs for planting and growing

- A minibeast hotel to attract small creatures that would otherwise not be drawn to the area

- Wheeled trolleys with stacked baskets for transporting resources between indoor and outside areas

- Sun-catchers and wind-chimes hanging from trees or shelters

- Pop-up tents for reading information books

Think about how the outdoor environment can be utilised to complement and extend the learning that is happening indoors.

- Sand and water trays to explore materials on a smaller yet still messy scale

- Hand held whiteboards, chalkboards and clipboards for children to record their thoughts and ideas.

No matter what size the outdoor area is the children should have free and open access to a range of resources so they can choose the things they need, helping them to independently sustain and develop their play. What's more, the layout should, as far as possible, be organised so the children have access to a variety of spaces that facilitate physical activity, as well as quiet play and conversation.

Don't forget to think about...

...planning outdoor experiences that complement and extend indoor learning. The resources and activities should capitalise on the unique nature of the outdoor environment. Plan activities that make the most of the space available and use the natural resources around you, and remember there is no need to restrict noise.

Collecting evidence of children's learning

The EYFS highlights observation as integral to teaching and learning. It is through observing children that practitioners get a rounded view of their interests, learning needs and attainment levels. The Framework states learning experiences should be shaped according to observation outcomes. Some children do most of their learning outside and it is just as important to observe outdoors as it is indoors.

Observing outdoors

Make observation outdoors as logistically possible as it is indoors. Ensure practitioners have the correct equipment to hand so they can carry out good quality observations when outside:

- Secure wall-mounted slings or wallets just inside the doorway leading out to the outdoor area. Use it to keep clipboards,

pens, post-it notes and cameras that practitioners can reach in and grab quickly when the need arises.

- Print off sheets of sticky labels for snap-shot observations. Design a template for each label with headings including, name of observer, date, time, name of child, area of learning and observation. These are quick to fill in and easy to transfer to assessment profiles.

- Fill waterproof bum bags with pens, post-its and digital cameras.

- Ensure every clipboard has a few plastic sleeves on it to protect notes from rain and messy play.

- Use dictaphones to record children's thoughts and comments as they play. This is more practical during messy physical activities that make holding a clipboard awkward.

Observation should be a fully inclusive process during which practitioners draw information from a variety of sources to gain a rounded view of the child. However, the EYFS acknowledges the burden of too much paperwork and stresses assessment should not be carried out at the expense of interacting with the children.

Bearing this in mind the example observation sheet on page 80 is designed to hold a large amount of information on a single document. There is space for recording the observation and assessment notes, as well as comments from other professionals, children and parents.

Observing and assessing science learning

When observing science exploration and investigation it is helpful to have a list of assessment questions to refer to. Either attach the list to your clipboard or include them on observation sheets (see the example on page 80) to help keep curriculum requirements in mind while observing. The list should help you to consider whether the children are:

- Able to identify objects, materials and living things

- Able to describe the features of objects, materials and living things

- Making comparisons and identifying similarities and differences

- Identifying links between different pieces of information

- Recording information using notes, pictures, diagrams and photos

- Asking questions and looking for answers

- Able to follow instructions

- Drawing on their knowledge and experience

- Coming up with ideas

- Able to clearly verbally express ideas and explain reasoning.

When observing an adult-led science activity it is helpful to observe with specific learning objectives in mind. There are different ways to do this. Either ensure the objectives are clearly stated in the planning and copy them onto observation sheets or include an assessment section on planning documents to record observation notes – also helpful for your own reflection upon how well the activity went.

Ensure practitioners have the correct equipment to hand so taking good quality observations is just as possible outside.

Assessing outdoor provision

Assess the use of outdoor space and resources by observing children's movements. This can be done through tracking observations, where practitioners focus on one child at a time and track their movements on a diagram of the outdoor area. The practitioner may either observe a child continuously for 10 minutes or for five minutes every 15 minutes over the course of an hour. They track the child's movements from one activity to the next and record how long the child remains at each. By choosing to observe a good cross section of children in one session practitioners can gain a clear picture of how well the outdoor space is working to suit particular needs and purposes.

Tracking observations can also be used to help practitioners assess how well subject-specific resources are working to enhance learning. This involves observing particular spaces and the use of resources instead of focusing on specific children. In the case of science, practitioners may choose to observe how well children make use of the sand and water resources. It might be that they continuously choose the funnels and jugs, ignoring the pipes and guttering, leading practitioners to consider what activities and challenges they can plan, as well as resources they can provide to get children making better use of this equipment.

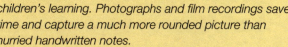

Don't forget to think about...

...using digital observations to capture snapshots of children's learning. Photographs and film recordings save time and capture a much more rounded picture than hurried handwritten notes.

Science observation record

Science observation record

Child's name:

Observer's name:

Area of provision/Focused activity:

Specific learning objectives:

Date:

Start time:

End time:

Observation notes:
Record here children's actions, comments and conversation.

Assessment questions:
Consider these questions in relation to the above observation.

Is the child…

Able to identify objects materials and living things?

Making comparisons and identifying similarities and differences?

Recording information using notes, pictures, diagrams and photos?

Able to follow instructions?

Coming up with ideas?

Able to describe the features of objects, materials and living things?

Identifying links between different pieces of information?

Asking questions and looking for answers?

Drawing on their knowledge and experience?

Able to clearly verbally express ideas and explain reasoning?

Assessment notes:

Implications for future planning:
Note down here any ideas stemming from this observation about investigations, activities or resources that build upon the findings of this observation.

Resources and further reading

Resources

- Telescopes (www.brightminds.co.uk)

- Pop-up tents, umbrellas, mini greenhouse, weathervane, bird table (www.reflectionsonlearning.co.uk)

- Sorting sets and containers, gardening tools, play tunnels, trikes, scooters, Magnetico, Sticklebricks, Mobilo, nuts and bolts, build and balance, stepping stones, crocodile rocker, windy playground sensory set, talking tubes, Tuff-Cam digital camera (www.eduzone.co.uk)

- Outdoor clothing, outdoor kitchen, garden workbenches, weather resistant learning boards, chalk boards, Smartmax, UR Tubes (www.earlyyearsdirect.com)

- Threading beads, gems and jewels, giant Polydron cogs and vehicle building sets, Big Gears construction set, marbling inks, Easi Speak microphones (www.earlyyearsresources.co.uk)

- Cork and dowel construction, mud kitchen, wide range of outdoor mark-making resources (www.playforce.co.uk)

- Wooden blocks, real building bricks, cork bricks, waterway and water wall sets, hollow building blocks, arch frames, willow wigwams, flower, bird, tree and minibeast identification cards (www.cosydirect.com)

- Minibeasts, dinosaur bones discover set, small world space set (www.yellow-door.net)

- Concave, convex and stretch and squash mirrors (www.morleysearlyyears.co.uk)

- Large and small hand-held metal detectors, Talking-Point recording devices, MP3 recorders, talking clipboards, child-friendly digital cameras, mini mobile phones, stethoscopes, hurdle stands, astronaut costumes, stomp rockets, squeeze rockets, safety goggles, Easi-scope magnifier, Tuff-Scope digital microscope, visualiser, Bee-bot, voice changer (www.tts-group.co.uk)

- Live bug and butterfly kits, bug viewers, wormery, grow your own lilypad kit, lifecycle posters (www.insectlore.co.uk)

- Ice ball makers, boat shaped silicone moulds, balsa wood aeroplane kits, waterproof chalk pens, novelty baking moulds, children's kites, crystal growing kits, camping stoves (www.amazon.co.uk) and (www.ebay.co.uk)

- Small polystyrene gliders (www.funlearning.co.uk)

- 2Simple computer software (www.2simple.com)

- Tizzy's First Tools computer software (http://shop.sherston.com)

Information books

- *All About Plants (Ways into Science)* by Peter Riley (Franklin Watts, 2014)

- *Big Book of Big Trucks* by Megan Cullis and Mike Byrne (Usborne, 2011)

- *British Wildlife: Hedgehogs* by Sally Morgan (Franklin Watts, 2008)

- *First Book of Ships and Boats* by Isobel Thomas (Bloomsbury, 2014)

- *How the Weather Works* by Christiane Dorion and Beverley Young (Templar, 2011)

- *I Wonder Why Planes Have Wings* by Christopher Maynard (Kingfisher, 2012)

- *Minibeasts (Little Science Stars)* by Jenny Vaughan (Ticktock, 2009)

- *RSPB First Book of Minibeasts* by Anita Ganeri, David Chandler and Mike Unwin (A&C Black, 2011)

- *See Inside Space* by Katie Daynes and Peter Allen (Usborne, 2008)

- *See Under the Sea* by Kate Davies and Colin King (Usborne, 2008)

- *Yucky Worms (Nature Storybooks)* by Vivian French and Jessica Ahlberg (Walker, 2012)

Resources and further reading

Further reading

- *50 Fantastic Ideas for Science Outdoors* by Kirstine Beeley (Featherstone, 2013)

- *Emergent Science* by Jane Johnston (Routledge, 2014)

- *Outdoor Learning in the Early Years: Management and Innovation* by Helen Bilton (Routledge, 2010)

- *Outdoor Play* by Sue Durant (Practical Pre-School Books, 2013)

- *Science 3-6: Laying the Foundations in the Early Years* edited by Max de Bóo (Association for Science Education, 2009). Accessed online: www.nationalstemcentre. org.uk/elibrary/resource/5973/science-3-6-laying-the-foundations-in-the-early-years

- *Science in the Early Years* by Pat Brunton and Linda Thornton (Sage, 2010)

- *Science Outdoors* by Christine Creamer (Lawrence Educational, 2007)

- *The Little Book of Explorations* by Sally Featherstone (Featherstone, 2010)

- *The Little Book of Investigations* by Sally Featherstone (Featherstone, 2013)

Useful websites

- Apps 4 Primary Schools: www.apps4primaryschools.co.uk

- Learning Through Landscapes: www.ltl.org.uk/

- Science Sparks: www.science-sparks.com

- Woodland Trust: www.naturedetectives.org.uk

- Royal Society for the Protection of Birds www.rspb.org.uk

References

Bilton, H. (2010) *Outdoor Learning in the Early Years: Management and Innovation*. Routledge, Oxon.

Bruner, J. (1966) *Toward a Theory of Instruction*. Harvard University Press, Cambridge, MA.

Council for the Curriculum, Examinations and Assessment (CCEA) (2006) *Northern Ireland Curricular Guidance for Pre-School Education*. CCEA, Belfast.

Council for the Curriculum, Examinations and Assessment (CCEA) (2007) *Northern Ireland Curriculum: Primary*. CCEA, Belfast.

Department for Children, Education, Lifelong Learning and Skills (DCELLS) (2008) *Foundation Phase Framework for Children's Learning for 3 to 7-year-olds in Wales*. DCELLS Publications, Cardiff.

Department for Children, Education, Lifelong Learning and Skills (DCELLS) (2008a) *Foundation Phase Framework: Learning and Teaching Pedagogy*. DCELLS Publications, Cardiff.

Department for Education (DfE) (2014) *Statutory Framework for the Early Years Foundation Stage*. DfE Publications, Nottingham.

Learning and Teaching Scotland (LTS) (2010) *Curriculum for Excellence through Outdoor Learning*. LTS, Glasgow.

Piaget, J. (1952) *The Origins of Intelligence in Children*. International Universities Press, New York.

Siraj-Blatchford, I., Sylva, K., Muttock, S., Gilden, R., Bell, D. (2002) *Researching Effective Pedagogy in the Early Years [REPEY]: Research Report No 356*. HMSO, London.

Siraj-Blatchford, I., Sylva, K., Melhuish, E., Sammons, P., Taggart, B. (2004) *Effective Provision of Pre-school Education [EPPE] Project: Final Report*. DfES, London and Institute of Education, University of London.

Sylva, K., Melhuish, E., Sammons, P., Siraj, I., Taggart, B., with Smees, R., Toth, K., Welcomme, W., Hollingworth, K. (2014) *Effective Pre-school, Primary and Secondary Education [EPPSE 3-16] Project: Research Report*. University of Oxford; Birbeck, University of London; Institute of Education, University of London.

Tickell, C. (2011) *The Tickell Review: The Early Years: Foundations for life, health and learning*. HMSO, London.

Vygotsky, L. (1986) *Thought and Language*. MIT Press, Cambridge, MA.

Notes